THE WALL
THAT HEALS

BY JAN SCRUGGS

With editorial assistance from
Kim Murphy

TABLE OF CONTENTS

FOREWORD

by Jan Scruggs

The Wall That Heals is a book that was written because it had to be written. More than 10 years have passed since ground was broken for the Vietnam Veterans Memorial in Washington, D.C. We now have a Memorial unlike any other in America or the world. Indeed, the Memorial has taken on religious significance for many. Some look on "The Wall" as more of a shrine than a monument. Like Mecca, the Wall beckons people to this sacred site where they can share their feelings and their pain at a place where—for many—their grief has been resolved. *The Wall That Heals* tells their story.

In 1969, I was a teenage infantryman with the U.S. Army in Vietnam. I was wounded in action in an infantry company which took high casualties. Serving my country was a difficult chore, but I was proud to do it. Back at home, I found my fellow veterans were being scorned for fighting in an unpopular war. Few people wanted to be reminded about the brave soldiers who died because their country asked them to serve. But the memories of my friends who gave their lives continued to haunt me.

Back in 1979, most people felt I was foolhardy to embark upon a journey to build a national Vietnam Veterans Memorial. I was told that a Memorial engraved with the names of those who died in Vietnam would never be built in Washington. Yet the sheer power of the idea seemed to overcome the incredible hurdles and seemingly insurmountable obstacles. Powerful opponents—including Members of Congress—had to be defeated at every stage. Looking back, it seems as though this is a Memorial that was just meant to be.

From the very beginning, my intention was to bring about a Memorial that would stand as a symbol of unity and reconciliation after the divisive Vietnam War. Those who took part in the Memorial's creation include General William Westmoreland, who once led U.S. troops into battle, and former Senator George McGovern, who once led the antiwar movement in the U.S. We reached out to all sides on the Vietnam controversy and now have a Memorial which serves as a bridge for an entire generation of Americans once divided over war.

In 1982, the Memorial was dedicated as a crowd of 150,000 people looked on. Since then, millions have been touched by a Memorial recognized internationally as a great work of art. The glory of that triumph belongs to Maya Ying Lin. While a college student in 1981, she created the simple yet powerful design that has moved so many people. This book is about some of those whose lives have been touched by this gentle, graceful Memorial.

You will be inspired by stories like that of Chuck Hagel, a decorated veteran who became President of the U.S.O. Kenneth Coskey's story of his four years as a POW in Vietnam is riveting. The tragedy of Wanda Ruffin, whose husband was missing in action until 1983, will make you understand the pain felt by those who wonder if their relatives will ever be found.

Some stories in this book will make you laugh. Others may make you cry. One thing is for sure—this book will make you think. It was partly luck to have found such a wonderful array of people to interview for this important book. The Vietnam Veterans Memorial, of course, is about people. People come there to honor those lost, to remember those who served. The millions of visitors who come each year to America's most-visited Memorial will never forget the experience.

In *The Winds of War*, Herman Wouk wrote, ". . .the beginning of the end of war is in remembrance. . ." Indeed, that's why this book is worth reading. The beginning of the end of the Vietnam War is reflected in the thoughts and feelings of those interviewed for this book.

I think Herman Wouk was right. And after reading this book, you too will likely agree. The beginning of the end of war *is* in remembrance.

INTRODUCTION

Days of rain had scattered puddles on sidewalks and in gutters lining Constitution Avenue. The air was cold. And still damp. The skies a sullen gray. Wind whistled through tightly wrapped jackets, swirling scarves melodically. Hundreds of thousands of people made their way down Constitution Avenue, heading towards a grassy knoll that lay between the Lincoln Memorial and Washington Monument.

It was Veterans Day, 1982. And the parade of men, women, and children were honoring the veterans who lost their lives in America's most divisive war. It was the dedication of the Vietnam Veterans Memorial.

As the crowd gathered behind the jagged, rust-colored fences, their eyes fixed upon the Memorial looming before them. The Wall. To the west, it started small, growing in size like a wave of blackness thundering through the ground. As it crested, it rolled gently to the east, diminishing in size, until it became a ripple that disappeared into the earth.

From a distance they could only see the silver glimmer of names. Their eyes squinted to read them from afar. As they did, many noticed that a silhouette of the gatherers was reflected in the Wall. Their mirrored expressions, tears, and wonderment melted among the sea of names.

The dedication speakers expressed their thoughts eloquently. They talked of great triumph. And everyone sang, God Bless America. Then the man whose vision it was to build the Wall, Jan Scruggs, spoke. "Ladies and Gentleman," he said victoriously, "the Vietnam Veterans Memorial is now dedicated."

A cheer rang through the crowd. The huddled mass began to press forward, eager to get closer. To see a name.

As people spotted their loved ones on the Wall, hands reached out, stretching to touch the names. Visitors couldn't get their gloves off fast enough. They wanted to feel the names against their skin. Fingers strained to caress the crisply-edged letters engraved in the black polished granite. The release of nearly two decades of suppressed pain and anger began to spill forth. That day, a nation began to heal.

The idea for the Vietnam Veterans Memorial first struck Jan Scruggs in March of 1979. He had just watched the *Deer Hunter*, a disturbing movie about the combat experience in Vietnam. Jan had served in Vietnam in 1969. He was wounded and decorated for bravery before he turned 20.

His vision seemed a lofty one. After all, it had taken decades for most Memorials to be approved and built. The idea for the Lincoln Memorial took 43 years to be approved by Congress. And Lincoln was very popular. Vietnam was not.

But Jan's idea for the Memorial was to honor the servicemen and women who had fought and who had died. Not to honor the war. Not to make a political statement about the war. He simply wanted to have those brave young people remembered. And give the estimated 43 million Americans directly affected by the casualties of Vietnam, a place to reflect, to mourn, and to heal.

He wasted no time recruiting supporters, most of them veterans themselves, although not all. They formed a non-profit organization, the Vietnam Veterans Memorial Fund, planned an aggressive timeline, and began their fundraising efforts. With the help of Senator Charles Mathias a spot of land near the Mall, between the Lincoln Memorial and the Washington Monument, was chosen as the future site of the Memorial.

At first money trickled in. But then they implemented a public awareness media campaign and the ball started rolling. Soon, donations were pouring in from mothers, fathers, brothers, sisters, widows, and girlfriends. Every penny came from the American public—not from the government. Americans did care about Vietnam vets after all.

In order to select a design for the Memorial, a panel of judges was recruited and a design competition announced. Each submission had to meet the following criteria: it had to be reflective and contemplative in character; it had to harmonize with its surroundings; it had to contain the names of those who had died in the conflict or who were still missing; and finally, the Memorial could not make a political statement about the war.

By the design deadline, March 31, 1981, the Fund had received 1,421 submissions. It was the largest number of entrees ever received in a design competition in the history of the country. One month later, the judging began. On May 1, the panel voted unanimously to award first prize to the design submitted by Maya Lin, a Yale University architecture student.

The design was unique. There was no other Memorial like it. Anywhere. It consisted of two walls, made of highly polished black granite, in a wide V-shape. Originally, each wall was to be 200 feet long. The east wall pointing to the Lincoln Memorial, the west pointing to the Washington Monument. The walls were to begin at ground level, gradually growing in size to 10 feet at the apex. The names of more than 58,000 dead and missing were to be engraved in the chronological order in which their lives were taken.

Controversy erupted almost immediately. The Fund went back through the submissions to confirm that the judging had been conducted properly. Again, Maya Lin's design won.

Throughout the construction planning phase, the debate waged on. At one point, all progress was halted. The Secretary of the Interior insisted that the Fund resolve the conflict before construction could begin. In January 1982, the Fund met with the opposition and reached a compromise. A more traditional statue and an American flag would be added at the Memorial site.

On March 26, 1982, the ground-breaking ceremony was held and construction began. For the next several months, crews worked tirelessly on inscribing the panels and placing them in the ground. An eight-foot-high fence kept curiosity seekers at bay. But construction workers often allowed families of killed veterans a glimpse of the structure. In less than eight months the Wall was completed. It came in on time and on budget.

The Vietnam Veterans Memorial is now a National Park Service site. But the Fund is still in existence. It is involved in organizing and sponsoring annual Memorial and Veterans Day ceremonies. This year it is focusing on plans for the 10th anniversary commemoration. The Fund is also concerned with the care and preservation of the Vietnam Veterans Memorial. In 1984, hairline cracks were noticed on one panel. In 1986, two panels were removed for inspection and reinstalled. The Fund also pays for all name changes, renovations, or additions made to the Memorial as well as other important needs. Today, there are more than 58,000 names inscribed on the Wall.

Since the dedication ceremony 10 years ago, streams of visitors have walked the Wall. Few, if any, who were originally opposed to the design feel the same way today. The Wall has taken on a power that even Jan Scruggs did not expect. Its power transcends description. It's an experience that must be felt to be understood.   In these pages, many people will try to describe that power. That experience. The people sharing their stories are the people most affected by the Wall. Veterans. Widows. Children of veterans killed. And the special people who give of their time and talents at the Wall, the volunteers. They share their stories courageously and lovingly so that others can better appreciate how the Wall heals the anguish caused by Vietnam.

I was very young during Vietnam. While the war spanned my formative years, I remember little. I remember wearing an MIA bracelet. Though I don't remember whatever happened to it. And I remember watching POWs step off the planes and onto American soil. For the most part however, my memories don't really kick in until sometime around Watergate.

So when I was hired to help write this book, I was intrigued. And ignorant. I didn't know how many men had been killed in Vietnam. And I had been to the Wall. I guess I never really thought about it. Or, if I did, it didn't stick with me. While I often wondered, "Whatever happened to the veterans who fought?" it never occurred to me that they were the ones coming into power in corporate America. Perhaps I believed a myth. The one that says Vietnam veterans are maladjusted, long hairs with scraggly beards. Oh sure, maybe some are. But there is a whole population of veterans out there who are clean-cut, well-adjusted, successful men.

In talking with these men, and with the families of men who died, I heard many descriptions of the Wall. One veteran, Kevin Finn, told me the design was appropriate because "Vietnam was like a scar." I also heard stories. I heard tales of people visiting the Wall for the first time who, for some odd reason, stopped arbitrarily in front of a panel and looked up only to see the very name they came to look for. Among 58,000 names that seems remarkable. Perhaps mythical. But then it happened to me.

The first time I visited the Wall was years ago. I found it breathtaking. Serene. Symbolic. But I knew no one on the Wall. For me, it was another monument. After conducting my interviews I felt compelled to go back. The Wall had taken on more meaning for me. I'd listened to heartfelt accounts of its power. Its ability to heal. I understood it better.

Yesterday, I went to the Wall. It's February now, and the cold winter wind is numbing. The sky was a milky gray. The color it turns before snow. In my pocket was a scrap of paper on which I had written down the names of the men I wanted to see. I knew exactly which panels they were on.

My eyes scanned the bottom right corner of each

panel looking for a number. I walked slowly. 36E. 37E. 41E. 42E. "This is it," I said. I lifted my head and my eyes focused. There it was. Instantly. The name I came to see. Jeffery Gurvitz. His name popped out, almost as if it were the only name on the Wall. I couldn't believe it. There were hundreds and hundreds of names on this panel. And yet, his was the first I saw. It was all I saw. I smiled. My heart was warmed. It seemed like a special moment. I can only imagine how special it seems to those who knew the person behind the name on which their eyes fall.

That is what is most important to remember. Behind every single name on that Wall there are people. People with stories. Memories. There is a family. A girlfriend. A widow. A child. There are combat buddies. Childhood friends. Roommates. And neighbors. There are teachers. Doctors. And coaches. Behind every single one of those 58,000 names stands a room full of people who remember.

Within these pages, is a handful of stories that detail how the Wall has touched their lives.

—*Kim Murphy*

Kim Murphy is a 1984 graduate of the University of North Carolina at Wilmington, with a Bachelor's Degree in Communications. She is a full-time freelance writer, who shares office space with her "private eye" husband in Falls Church, Virginia. They live in Manassas with their 10-year-old dog, Mac, and cockatiel, Pumpkin.

MIKE KENTES

If Mike Kentes hadn't been drafted, he would have volunteered to go to Vietnam. He grew up in a military family. His father was a career soldier who had fought in Vietnam. His older brother also fought in Vietnam. Joining the military was a natural progression, like getting your driver's license. . .buying your first car. . .or drinking a beer before you turned of age.

"I wanted to be a soldier," he says proudly. And you believe him. "I wanted to be a paratrooper in the infantry," he continues. And again, you believe him. Although the military had a hard time believing it at the time.

"No one wants to be in the infantry," they told him, as they led him before a board of psychiatrists to make sure his mind was all there.

"I never thought it would be so hard to get into the infantry," he laughs.

Once accepted, Mike went to infantry training. It was 1968. . .at the height of the war. After infantry training at Fort Ord, California, and paratrooper training at Fort Benning, Mike was selected to go to pathfinders school. Pathfinders concentrate on map reading and guide airborne drops. "We would parachute in first," he describes, "set up the drop zone, and guide the planes in. For the Vietnam War, we were concentrating on air mobile operations, guiding in helicopters, and clearing landing zones, things like that."

By April 1969, he was off to Vietnam. "I was assigned to the 9th Infantry Division. Originally I was assigned to a pathfinder detachment that was assigned to the 9th Aviation Battalion, which was a helicopter battalion. But we weren't doing much and I found out about the LRRP (Long Range Reconnaissance Patrol). It was right across the street. So I went over and volunteered for the LRRPs, or the Rangers as they were called."

It took a while for Mike's orders to come in, but after about a month he was assigned to the LRRPs. He was in the E Company, 50th Infantry, which was later changed to E Company, 75th Rangers.

On his third mission, there were six on his team conducting a parakeet flight. In a parakeet flight, a team flies a light observation helicopter, or lurch, with a mini-gun and two gunships. Their mission was to conduct a quick raid on an area—to find the enemy "with their pants down." It was an effective strategy. But it was also risky. "We got a lot of kills on those type missions," Mike says, "but we got a lot of guys killed as well."

The team leader was a man named "Dan" D. His real name was Curtis, but his buddies called him Dan. Mike V. was the team's point man. Team leaders were chosen not by rank but by who had the most experience and was the best in the field. The team leader communicated with the helicopters above using a radio. The point man led the team through the jungle. It was considered one of the most dangerous jobs. The point man was always the most vulnerable. Vulnerable to tree limbs rigged with grenades—poised to explode at just the slightest touch—and to Viet Cong lurking behind bushes waiting to assault.

On this particular night, the VC were ready. In seconds, Dan and Mike were shot and killed. Poncho lay wounded. His arm ripped open, raw and bleeding. Now the team had three men left fighting, Mike, Marty F., and Bill C.

Unfortunately, the bullet that killed Dan had also shattered the communication radio. Most nights, the team had two radios. This night, there was only one.

"We had no communication with the helicopter above," Mike remembers. "It was circling above. About that time, our Lieutenant flipped out, picked up Dan's weapon and started shooting at our own helicopter. Bill grabbed him—he was the Sergeant—and said, 'What the hell are you doing?!' Finally the lurch came down, and Bill ran across the rice paddy to inform them what the situation was."

In war, you never leave your buddies. If they die on the battle field, you go back in to get them. It's an unspoken pledge. "They landed on the ground and we all got together. He [the pilot] said, 'Well do you want to go get them [the bodies]?' We thought all three of them were dead. Poncho wasn't moving. We looked at him and said, 'Of course we want to go get the bodies.' So we got on line and we assaulted."

The remaining team members made their way back in the jungle to retrieve their friends. "When we got there, we found out that Poncho was still alive. So, we got him back and loaded him on the lurch. Marty and Bill drug Dan's body out while I stayed with Mike's body 'til they could return. While I was sitting there, I looked up and saw the Viet Cong. He was smiling, looking through the bush at me. I shot him. And then Bill and Marty came assaulting back when they heard me shooting." The three men carried out their friend, climbed into the lurch, and headed back to prepare for their next mission.

On another mission, Mike was wounded in the leg by some burnt shrapnel. "When I went in the aid station," he says, "there were guys laying around all shot up, and I just, you know I had a burnt leg, and it just wasn't that bad. So, I got some medication and got the hell out of there."

Listening to his stories, Mike sounds the epitome of a rough and tumble kind of guy. Boisterous. Brave. And bawdy. "I was gung-ho, and a lot of times that didn't go over well with a lot of the other troops," he admits. "But that's why I joined the LRRP unit. I wanted to be around guys who were into it."

After his tour of duty was complete, Mike returned to New Jersey. But nothing had prepared him for what faced veterans when they returned home.

"As soon as I walked in the airport this little hippy spit at me. I had my greens on and she spit at me. This old guy walked up and slapped her. And he says, 'I've never struck a woman before in my life, but I saw her do that.' And, I mean, he belted her. I thought, 'What the hell is going on?' It turned out the old guy was with the Marines in World War II at Iwo Jima. Then a policeman came up and arrested her. And I kept saying, 'What the hell is going on?'"

Part of Mike's confusion was that while in Vietnam he hadn't realized the extent of the protests in the States. In fact, he says, "Hell, I thought we were winning the war."

Mike shrugged off the incident and continued to make his way through the airport. It was early 1970. An air traffic controllers strike was heating up. There were lines and lines of people at every counter.

"I'm at the back of the line and the counter clerk says, 'Son, you just get back from Vietnam?' I said, 'Yeah.' And he said, 'Come on up here.'" Mike pauses while telling the story. He looks up at the ceiling in an effort to blink back the tears. "This gets emotional," he says apologetically. "Then the people started applauding. And he put me ahead of the line. It was really neat. But, it was really, really confusing."

Today, Mike is in his early 40s. But in 1970, he was still just a kid. A kid who had gone off to war. The impact on his life that year in combat resonated over the next two decades. If being at war was hard, being at home sometimes seemed harder.

"It truly was the first war where I think the soldiers had to buy the beer when they came back. Basically you wanted to talk about it. Hey, we had done some exciting things over there. I mean sitting in a helicopter going 90

MPH, 20 feet above the ground, with gun ships blaring next to you and artillery coming in. Being in fire fights and seeing some pretty traumatic stuff. You know, you wanted to talk about it. But you soon found out real quick, that you damn well better not talk about it.''

"Then you started hearing stuff like 'Oh, you were in Vietnam. You must have been really stupid because anybody who is smart is smart enough to go to college or evade the draft or whatever.' That really ticks you off. So you just start shutting up about it—and I've got a pretty big mouth anyhow," he laughs at himself for a moment. "But then they'd start ridiculing you and the guys you served with. The men I served with over there, except for a few exceptions, were some of the finest people I ever met. And they weren't loony before they went over either. That was another thing. Guys started having all these problems because they had been through a lot, and they couldn't talk about it. But people started saying they were just crazy before they went over."

The adjustment for many veterans, including Mike, was difficult—in love, at work, and at play. Mike says, "I had so many jobs. And I wasn't lazy. I'd get fired. I guess after you've been through combat—and I've heard this from Korean and World War II vets, too—you have a hard time putting up with Mickey Mouse stuff on the job."

It was also a rude awakening to learn the real world didn't possess the comraderie of war.

"When you're in any combat unit, you get so close. . . if you needed money, a guy would loan you money. He'd give you the shirt off his back. We thought the whole world was like that because we were at such an impressionable age. Then you get back here, and it ain't that way."

Then, there are the personal emotions veterans suffered—almost always in silence. The anger. The depression. The sorrow. "I'd go in a rage, getting mad real easy...a real short fuse. That's why guys lost so many jobs or couldn't keep a job. You can only cuss your boss out so many times—or punch him—before you lose your job."

Those who could no longer suffer in silence sometimes chose to end their lives. "Fortunately, I've never had any suicidal tendencies. We just lost another Ranger about a year ago. He committed suicide," Mike says quietly.

These are the pains felt by combat veterans. These are the wounds the Wall helps mend. "I thought it was a beautiful design," Mike remembers thinking when he first heard about the Memorial. "One of the frustrating things about hearing all the protests and the insults was that nobody was talking about Dan and Mike...and you know, Frosty, he was killed...and Lamb...and the guys who were wounded. No one was talking about them. So, when they dedicated that Wall, boy, it was great. But they could have rolled a big rock out there, put the names on it, and I would have been happy."

Mike attended the dedication ceremonies for the Wall. Standing in front of the panel where his buddies' names were etched, Mike said the Lord's Prayer as he held a single red carnation against the panel's seam. "Their names were too high up the Wall, so I couldn't touch them. But I stood looking at them while I prayed."

The impact of the Wall on Mike's ability to let go of the guilt, grief, and anger is immeasurable. "I can sleep now at night. It used to take me—this is like a miracle—it used to take me two hours a night to get to sleep. I could not sleep. I didn't have nightmares so to speak, but I would always reenact a battle I was in, before I would go to sleep. And it would take two hours. After they dedicated that Wall, I mean, I could fall right to sleep," he says, still somewhat amazed.

For veterans, Mike believes the Wall was the long overdue recognition they deserved. "Hey, we were a good body of soldiers and sailors and airmen over there. I mean, we fought a damn good war, I thought, considering the parameters we had to work under. Especially since most of us were like 18 or 19 years old . . .with a company commander who's only 23," he stops, thinks for a moment then shakes his head. "I help coach the George Mason University rugby team now, and I look at these guys who are 22, you know, and I just go 'God, they're so young.'"

"I went over for the dedication, with my wife and son. It was great. Just being around all those guys again, it was like being back in Vietnam with your buddies. In 1984, when they dedicated the statue, myself and Tom set up a LRRPs and Rangers reunion. We rented a room at a hotel and put out notices. We had about 150 guys show up from different divisions, not just ours. But we all had the same mentality and bent. We went down to the Wall together on Saturday, and hung out in the room all weekend. We even went back [to the Wall] on Sunday."

Mike describes the empathy he felt that weekend. "The first day it was really hard to get down to the Wall because there were so many people. There were a lot of parents and widows there. They're the ones I felt most sorry for. I never realized how much they went through until I had a son. And then you start looking at him and wondering, 'What would I do if I lost him?' And whether it's your son or daughter makes no difference, it's your child."

The dedication of the Wall gave veterans "permission" to talk about the things they'd held inside for so long. As they talked, the others began to better understand their struggles. The Wall helped bring together a nation that had been divided. It brought together families. And friends.

"I noticed people started asking me more about Vietnam. When I went to George Mason University to coach, I found the students were a real patriotic bunch. They'd say, 'Ah, you're a Vietnam veteran. . .Will you talk about it?' I think building the Wall helped bring us back together. The phone company must have made a fortune after that Wall was dedicated because guys just started calling each other up. I called up as many of the parents as I knew of the guys who were killed. I wouldn't get into any gory details, they don't need that, but many of the parents wanted to know more about how their son died. And I always told them how brave their sons were."

Mike, and many others, have made new friends at the Wall as well. "One time," he says, "a guy walked up to me, and said this long sentence in a foreign language. It was Ukrainian. I said, 'I understand what it means, but I can't speak Ukrainian.'" Apparently, the man could tell that Mike was of Ukrainian descent. "I said, 'How did you know?' And he said, 'I can look at you.' Then, he said, 'What do you do for work?' This was in '82, and I was unemployed. He said, 'Well give me your name and number.' Two months later he called me up, and he had a job for me." That man who uttered those Ukrainian words was also named Mike. This Mike is 6 foot 4 inches and 250 pounds. He is of Mongolian descent with Oriental features and coloring. They called him the Mongol. When the two Mikes are together, Kentes jokes that he found Mike M. in the jungles of Vietnam, brought him back to the states, and civilized him.

In truth, Mike M. is also a Vietnam veteran. He was with the Wolf Hounds 25th Infantry division when they left Hawaii by boat. His company ran into a North Vietnamese regiment totaling nearly 600 men. Kentes tells Mike's story. "There were probably like 150 of our guys against 600 of theirs. We killed a lot of the enemy. But from that one day, Mike knows 35 names in a row on the Wall."

When Kentes tells this story, you can tell meeting Mike

at the Wall was a turning point in his life. It was a moment that spawned a treasured friendship. Even more important, someone had reached out to help. A veteran helping another veteran. As if he were saying, "Here's the shirt off my back." It was a gesture that restored one man's sense of self-esteem, pride, and faith in others. His soul was healed.

PEGGY BORSAY

Widow of Peter Borsay

It was Christmas, 1967. Peggy and Peter Samuel Borsay were being married at the Washington National Cathedral. She was 21 years old, he was 22. Peggy wore a soft, white velvet dress. It enhanced her petite 5'1'' frame. Peter, who loved to wear classic, stylish clothes, wore a crisply pressed formal tuxedo. Smiling, she whispered the words, "I, Peggy, take you Peter. . .until death us do part." She never imagined that years later she'd find herself sitting in those very same church pews, listening, stoically, as Peter's name was read aloud during the dedication ceremonies for the Vietnam Veterans Memorial.

Peter's family had fled Budapest, Hungary, in 1947, and lived in Canada for 10 years before emigrating to the United States. In the mid-1960s, he became a U.S. citizen. When he was drafted, Peter was working on his PhD and teaching at the University of Utah. Thoughts crossed his mind about fleeing to Canada. But America had been a land of hope and opportunity for him and his family. And while fighting didn't sound like the best idea, he was sure he didn't want to live his life as a fugitive. In April 1969, after basic training and AIT training at Fort Ord, California, Peter left for Vietnam.

It was only weeks later, on May 31, 1969, that Peter was killed by a short rocket round—an American rocket that had fallen "short" of its target. It was Memorial Day. He was only 24 years old.

"Before he left, he told me if I got a telegram not to be worried because that meant that he was wounded. But if I saw someone coming to the door, then I would know he had been killed. And so of course when I saw the man at the door, I knew exactly what had happened," Peggy recalls.

Peggy reeled from the news. "How could this be?" she wondered. We had so many hopes...so many dreams...such a long list of things we wanted to do together. "How in the world can this be happening to me?" she must have questioned.

"At 22, I was making arrangements for my husband's funeral," Peggy says. "I had never even attended a funeral before. My image of a widow was a woman with gray hair, and stooped shoulders, after 40 or 50 years of marriage."

Peggy recalls some of the difficult decisions she had to make in those first few days after she heard the news. "When Peter's body came back from Vietnam, I had the choice whether to have the funeral be open casket or closed casket. I chose to have a closed casket. He was not maimed in any way, but I chose not to look at his body. I think I just couldn't accept the fact that he was gone. And I can remember in the funeral home, sitting all alone in a room with his casket closed, just sobbing, but not being able to look inside that casket. It was a mistake. I should have [looked], because instead, I was able to deny for a very long time that he was gone."

Much of Peggy's denial of Peter's death was facilitated by her work at Walter Reed Army Medical Center. There, Peggy accepted a position as an education-vocational counselor. Walter Reed was the primary orthopedic hospital for the Army. Many of the amputees from Vietnam went to Walter Reed before being transferred to a hospital closer to their home. Because of the thousands of men needing medical attention, Walter Reed had large open wards with two rows of beds. For Peggy, that meant she was able to hunt and hope, however subconsciously, that she might one day find Peter in one of the beds on the wards.

"In 1969 and '70," Peggy explains, "we were at the height of the war. So there would be incredible numbers of men coming in from Vietnam and they'd be lined up out in the hallways. We'd have so many men. And they just kept coming. Even if somebody left, there was always somebody to fill that bed.

"I was able to say to myself that they might have made a mistake. . .that he could be alive," she says. "And every time a new shipment of men came in I would always be over there right away. I don't consciously remember looking for Peter, but I remember looking for his dark curly hair, and the shape of his head, or somebody who had his features. I remember for years after he was killed, if I would see anyone walking down the street who looked like him, [I would go] running after that person. I'm sure it was because I simply didn't look at his body [in the casket]."

And then there was the guilt. "Part of the guilt, for me," Peggy says, "is that it was of course Memorial Day weekend and I had spent the entire weekend by the pool playing bridge and having a good time while they were looking for me to tell me that he had been killed. And so literally, for years and years afterwards, it was hard for me to have a good time. . .because I had been having a good time when he was dead."

Because Vietnam was such a source of conflict, widows and returning veterans routinely kept their pain to themselves. They suffered in isolation. In silence. Peggy was no exception. She has struggled with her pain over Peter's death for over 20 years.

"I had never met or talked to another Vietnam widow before about a year ago," Peggy says. "Think of the isolation involved in that. And think of the veterans. . .there are so many memories that they have never talked about. I mean, if I never talked about being a widow until recently they certainly have never talked about the experiences that they had in Vietnam.

"Certainly, Vietnam widows who were part of a military community had many more opportunities to come in contact with other Vietnam widows," Peggy says. "But many of us—wives of men who were drafted—never came in contact with each other."

Even as late as 1982, when Peggy attended the dedication ceremonies for the Wall, she had not met other widows. In fact, she had no interest or desire to meet other widows for fear of the feelings she might experience. She believed—albeit incorrectly—that she had already healed much of her pain.

"I thought at that time, 'Okay, now I'm going to do this [participate in the dedication events] and then I'll be fine. I'll be able to get on with my life.' But actually that was, for me anyway, only the beginning of the process of healing."

Peggy captured her first thoughts about the Wall on tape during her visit to the dedication ceremonies. Her thoughts are featured in the next chapter. She still remembers being amazed at how quiet people were as they walked beside the Wall.

"And that is no different today. . . people are still very quiet," Peggy says. "It's a very hushed kind of atmosphere. I think it is the perfect design. It honors the men who died there, but doesn't honor war. In fact, it makes very visible for everyone who sees it, the cost of war in very real terms. . . because it's name after name after name. It's somebody's brother or father or husband. I can't imagine any other way that you can really see the cost of war in such a concrete way.

"For me, there is comfort in knowing that permanently and publicly there is some place where Peter's name is. He had an incredible impact on people's lives, and they do remember him. Even today, people will write to me and say, 'I was at the Memorial. I looked up Peter's name. I touched his name' or 'I made a rubbing of it.' Even my friends—friends that I have met since Peter was killed, who never knew him—will look up his name and touch it. It's as if he lives on and people remember that it wasn't just some stranger who was killed in

Vietnam . . . it was real people, and it was Peter."

Ironically, though she had no interest in communing with others who suffered as she had, it was her experiences with the Wall that prompted Peggy not only to meet other widows, but also to seek them out. In the late 1980s, she started The Vietnam Widows Research Project in an attempt to network with other widows, research, and study the ways these women were coping with the loss of their husbands.

"Getting to a point where I could talk about all those feelings, and even remembering all those feelings, took a long time. One of my greatest fears in beginning the Vietnam Widows Research Project was that I knew that if I was to be effective at doing that research I was going to have to share my feelings as well. It meant reliving that pain and revisiting that pain over and over again. I wasn't sure I had the strength. I wasn't sure I could do that."

Enabling people to talk about their pain, sorrow, and experiences is one of the greatest contributions the Wall has made to several generations of people—from the parents of the young men who were killed to their now fully grown children. As Peggy began to become more comfortable with the idea of talking about her personal experience, she realized she was ready to reach out to other Vietnam widows. Of the more than 58,000 men who were killed, 17,000 left behind a widow who had to carry on in spite of her despair. And there were also the girlfriends and fiancees whose pain has been forgotten.

Peggy and her partner, Jacquelyn Beattey, decided one of the easiest ways to find other widows was to go to the Wall. On Memorial Day weekend in 1990, they set up an information table at the Wall. For Peggy, this was truly a monumental step. Not only was she venturing out, knowing she was putting herself at risk of experiencing a wealth of emotions, but she was also going to be visiting the Wall on the anniversary of her husband's death. It had, at that point, been 21 years since Peter had been killed. Although sometimes, for Peggy, the pain cut so deep it seemed like only yesterday she heard the news. But the fact that she persevered in her mission to find other widows proved she was one step closer to being at peace.

She describes her activities that weekend. "We went on Saturday to set up the table. I mean, we had, literally, a card table with two lawn chairs and a sign that said Vietnam Widows Project. We had a stack of these fact sheets, with our cards on the table. And that was it. We were there Saturday, Sunday, and Monday. . . it had to be the hottest Memorial Day weekend in memory. So, we just baked out in the sun."

During the course of those three days, Peggy and Jacki spoke with several veterans and children of men killed in action. Unfortunately, they met only two widows.

"We met one widow who had come from California to see the Wall for the first time. Her daughter had given her the ticket to come to the Wall for Memorial Day as a gift," Peggy recalls. "We had an incredible number of children of Vietnam widows who stopped and said, 'I'd like to take your information to my mom.' And as we talked with them, I began to realize that my experience in not talking about being a Vietnam widow was not unusual. . .a lot of Vietnam widows still hadn't [talked about it]. But their children recognized that they needed to."

Perhaps the most pleasant surprise Peggy discovered, as she met more and more people at the Wall, was the unspoken bond she felt when talking with veterans.

"There is an instantaneous bond between a Vietnam widow and a veteran that I wasn't aware of before. It's as though there is a combination of guilt—because they lived and my husband didn't—and a combination of incredible caring and protectiveness. They'd say, 'If you ever need anything, you know we're here.' And there were spontaneous hugs. For these rough and tumble guys, it's just amazing to me that there is that much emotion for someone they have never met before. And these aren't men who knew my husband, but they knew other men just like my husband."

Over the last 10 years, Peggy has visited the Wall numerous times during her five trips to the Washington area.

"It always brings me to tears," she says, "in a way that nothing else can. I don't know if I could articulate exactly why. . . but I think it comes from a culmination of feelings around the loss, the sadness at the things that Peter was unable to do, that he wanted so much to do. The fact that his name is surrounded by so many other names, and they knew people like me who feel the same way. Each time I have been there, I've watched veterans as they touch a buddy's name or just stand quietly with tears running down their cheeks."

"I think for me and for many others who lost someone in Vietnam, the Wall is significant in that it wasn't something that the government put up. It was something that people who cared about those who died in Vietnam did. And for me, part of that significance is that a very small piece of that Wall was supported by my money. I am a part of what has become a place where people can remember. So I feel a real personal ownership in that. And each time I go and see the number of people who are there, young and old and in between, it becomes another part of the healing process for me."

Peggy believes that while her healing continues, she is slowly finding a greater sense of peace. She plans to attend the commemoration events on the 10th anniversary of the Wall this November. Peggy says she hopes this visit to the Wall "will provide a closure to the sharpness of the pain around losing Peter in Vietnam. It will be more of a fond remembering. And a deeper feeling of acceptance.''

MEMORIES FROM THE WALL

Peggy Borsay first visited the Vietnam Veterans Memorial during the dedication ceremonies in November 1982. She also participated in the name-readings at the Washington National Cathedral. To help heal the pain of her husband's death, Peggy tape recorded her thoughts during those few days. She was kind enough to share this very personal and private journal of her feelings and reflections with me. Here are excerpts from her original tape.

Veterans Day. . .and the time of the National Salute to Vietnam Veterans. I'm in Washington, D.C., for that occasion which started yesterday with the reading of the names of men killed in Vietnam, almost 58,000 of them. The names are being read around the clock. Peter's name was read sometime between 2:15 and 2:45 yesterday afternoon. At around 2:00, I read a prayer for Vietnam veterans and 10 of the names of men who had been killed.

This candlelight vigil is being held at the Washington National Cathedral which is where Peter and I were married—almost 15 years ago—on December 27, 1967. I was dressed in white velvet and he was dressed in a fancy tuxedo. And we were happy. It didn't take long for all that to change.

I was struck yesterday by the quiet way in which people came to hear a name read. They sat quietly and heard that name. They had a few tears. . . or, sometimes none at all. And then they left just as quietly as they had come. A constant stream of people coming and going. All very quiet, all very subdued. No fanfare. Basically people came and went and expressed their grief in a very quiet, private kind of way.

I saw a couple of uniforms, Army uniforms. I saw a lot of Vietnam veterans, some of them dressed in suits and ties and white shirts. Some of them dressed in jeans and plaid flannel shirts. Some of them with jeans and knapsacks and long straggly beards. They seemed to know who was a veteran and who wasn't. I overheard scraps of conversations reminiscing about where they had been in Vietnam...and what unit they had been with.

There were mothers and fathers...sisters and brothers...and men who had served in Vietnam...all who had come to show they remembered those men who didn't come home from the war.

I heard an elderly couple come in. He had on an overcoat and blue hat. She was dressed in a coat and scarf and warm hat. They asked if it would be safe for them to come back at 2:00 in the morning, when their son's name would be read. The woman who was coordinating the candlelight vigil was so kind to them. She told them that they could park very close and that she would walk them back to their car. They wanted to know what was on the white pieces of paper that people were carrying around. She told them it was the prayers that would be read every 15 minutes. Without them even having to ask, she asked them if they would like a copy of those prayers. They said "yes." They keep a book for their son of all the things about him...all those things which affected him.

For me, it was very much like when Peter had first been killed. I would be fine one minute and the next minute I would be dissolving in tears...never knowing when it was going to hit me, never knowing when I would be out of control again. When I got to the last couple of names that I read, my voice was breaking and I wasn't sure I was going to be able to finish it. Then, we sat and listened to name after name after name being read. When they came to Peter's name, I sat like a statue afraid to allow myself to feel the pain and the loneliness and the anger that's brewed for almost 13 years.

It felt good to be able to talk about it . . . to be able to talk about how I feel. I suppose it feels good, too, to know that there are other people who are also grieving. People who cry silent tears for somebody they miss, too. Somebody, I figured, nobody else remembered was gone.

I suppose, too, it's time to allow myself to cry again.

I think now, by allowing myself to feel these emotions, talk about them, and think about them, some kind of healing process is going on. Maybe I'll be able to close the wound and put the salve on to help it heal.

In other ways, it feels like when Peter was first killed. Other people are going on with their lives. For a few days the Vietnam veterans will be all over the news. And then they'll be forgotten again. Maybe not so much now. Maybe some things will change for them and for me. And maybe through that process a lot of people can begin to move on with their lives . . . including me.

November 13, 1982

It's November 13, 1982, and today the Vietnam Memorial was dedicated in downtown Washington, D.C. I was there, with my brother Steve, and what looked to be hundreds of thousands of other people . . . veterans in fatigues . . . men in Army uniforms . . . women in Army, Air Force, Navy, and Marine uniforms. Men carrying banners with the names of states on it. Men carrying flags with the names of different units. Crudely painted signs with the names of units and directions to a reunion party. Snatches of conversation as we walked to the Memorial told of men reliving old battles or reminiscing about R&R times in various exotic places.

There was a whole section devoted to handicapped men, and once again I saw men in wheelchairs with no legs. I saw men on crutches with one leg. I saw men without arms . . . with eye patches on . . . with vacant stares. It was just as I used to see day after day at Walter Reed... the beds filled up, men left or died, and still the beds were filled.

Parents, older people, small children, young children, everybody coming to the Memorial to remember someone. Park police on their horses... and on their mopeds. Thousands and thousands of people walking towards a Memorial made of black granite with almost 58,000 names carved into it.

Because I was a widow, we had special badges that got us into a reserved area. We were very close to the Memorial and able to see most everything that was going on. The Marine Corps band was playing background music. There were lots of people with cameras trying to take pictures of the panel on which their loved one's name appeared. There were speeches... prayers... a thanksgiving... a welcoming home... and a remembering of those who would never be welcomed home. One of the ministers who prayed talked of the need to let go of the pain and the guilt... to remember the good times, remember the love making, and the happiness... to use this time to let go.

After the service was over, we walked up along the Wall to find Peter's name. We had to stop and ask a little old lady with white hair where it would be. She looked it up in the book. His name is on Panel 23 west, the 26th line down. Steve saw it first. It took me a long time to find it. It was difficult to see his name on that Wall... to know that he would be one of those 58,000. And to know, when people walk along it, they might never pick his name out as a special name. Only those of us who loved him and still remember him will look for his name.

It was a hard day. It was cold and it was windy. The ground was very wet from rain... and muddy. The sun would come out periodically. A kite was flying high in the air with an American flag attached to it.

There was a sense of patriotism and a sense of righting

a wrong...of making the fact that those men served in Vietnam not something to apologize for anymore.

It was a day filled with emotion, sadness, tears, and tiredness. Tonight, that's my overwhelming feeling, just a sense of tiredness. But somewhere deep inside I also feel that the healing can now begin, in a way that I could never let Peter go before. Before, I would never believe when I looked at the headstone on his grave that he was really dead. Now I can believe it and, in a way, that lets the pain not be so bad anymore.

CHUCK HAGEL

In her book, *Long Time Passing* (1984, Doubleday), Myra McPherson gives a chilling account of the combat experience in Vietnam. Here is an excerpt from her chapter, "Two Soldiers":

The patrol picked its way through jungle so thick that by noon it was dark. A dead, midnight kind of darkness. Fifty men threaded their way. The first 10 began to cross a river. The soldier walking point touched something with his boot. It was not a twig, not a root, not a rock. It was a trip wire to oblivion. In an instant the wire triggered a huge, fifty-pound Chinese mine. There was an enormous roar, like the afterburner of a jet, as it exploded, instantly ripping the point man apart. Shrapnel flew for yards.

Tom, six feet tall and slim, at 19 already developing a characteristic slouch, froze, hunched his shoulders, and in a flash, caught the scene forever in his mind: the face of one buddy disintegrating from the explosion; others walking their last steps and falling, bones sticking white out of flesh sheared off at the hips. Some bled to death, coating the ground and mud and leaves with their last moments of blood, before the medevac choppers could come. Some were caught in the river. Tom always remembers the river, running red "like Campbell's tomato soup." Those that weren't hit screamed in panic. Those that were screamed in pain.

Tom's first thought, as always, was of Chuck. He whipped around and saw Chuck lying immobile, staring, with the most startled look Tom had ever seen on his face.

Tom wasn't sure what was causing it—Chuck's breathing or his heartbeat—but something was causing it. Every few seconds, a fountain of blood gushed from a wound in Chuck's chest. Tom knelt and, with trembling fingers, grabbed a compression bandage, a thick cotton square with the bandage tied to it like a scarf. He wrapped one, two, three around Chuck's chest, pulling tight. The pressure held back the gush, even though blood seeped out around the borders—a brilliant Pop Art pattern—but the bandages held.

Only then did Tom feel something sticky on his left arm. He felt down around his elbow. His hand came back bloody. A chunk of shrapnel was lodged there. Someone quickly bandaged his arm.

There was no time for anything but frantic, adrenaline-charged action. The jungle growth was so thick that they had to hack fiercely at the bamboo, its sharp ridges ripping their skin, before the medevac helicopters could come in. The choppers took the seriously wounded—the ones with no legs, the ones with gaping chests. And the dead. More than 15 of the men were dead or seriously wounded.

The rest would simply have to walk out of there.

Only later would Tom and Chuck have time to think that magic was with them once again. They almost always walked point—one checking for snipers and grenades and booby traps, the other following right behind with compass and map.

They had been walking point all morning. Just five minutes before the explosion, the captain had decided to rotate his troops. Had they been walking point, they would have been dead.

For those left in the jungle, the terror of the next hours would rival the horror of the mine going off. They were in the kind of war America's youth fought without end in Vietnam—an unceasing guerilla war with an enemy seldom seen. A kind of war perfected by the VC...a kind of war that to this day brings shaking nightmares to many veterans...

"We had to move off the trail and chop our way

out—every step of the way," remembers Tom. "The reason we got blown up, to begin with, is that we walked on the trail."

The jungle was steaming—as if the sky was not sky at all but a giant bell jar encasing some monstrous greenhouse. The men gulped for air, but suffocated in the humidity. Sweat and blood stuck to backs, arms, legs. No one knew if the mine was a prelude to an ambush. There was always the certain knowledge that the Vietnamese knew that jungle like the back of their hands, that they could walk it blindfolded at night.

Something as ominous as a lurking enemy was at hand: hundreds of grenades, lightly attached by thin, invisible wires, festooned the jungle growth like deadly hidden ornaments on a tree. The least snag of a foot would trip a wire, pull the pin, and the spoon would fly off. Just brushing against a tree could set the grenades off. After what they had seen, there was enormous fear. With each step, they waited for the sound of an explosion, a scream of pain. It took four hours to go 500 yards. "Every 20 feet you would run into another booby trap," recalls Chuck. "The options were either to go around a grenade, once you spotted it, or try to disarm it, stick the pin back in if you could. There were some guys that shouldn't have messed with them and did. They got their arms blown off."

Tom's voice shakes. "We just prayed we'd get the hell out of there." Some men would get very, very quiet. Some would cry. Everyone could feel the gut panic. "All you could do was hold to the back strap of the one in front when it gets that dark. You couldn't keep spirits up, couldn't talk loud for fear the VC were around."

Tom's eyes grow distant. "It was one of the most terrible times."

Chuck is 37 now. Tom 35. In 1980, they came together for a singularly compelling reunion. There were disagreements and raised voices as they sifted through the endless maze that was Vietnam, but through it all there was a palpable, protective, and unshakable love. For Chuck and Tom have know each other a long time.

Tom's earliest memory of Chuck: the two of them sitting on a dusty curb in their jockey shorts in a small Nebraska town. Two little boys talking with some friends as early morning summer sun washed the Nebraska sandhills. A woman comes out and tells them, "For land's sake! Go in and put some clothes on." Tom, age three, toddles in after Chuck, age five.

Tom and Chuck are brothers.

The Hagel brothers look amazingly untouched by the war, although shrapnel still floats in Chuck's chest and Tom's back is dotted with little scars and darker, pitted spots.

Years later, little metal reminders of Vietnam have their way of working their way out of the system. One night recently, Tom woke to find one side of his neck, near his ear, severely swollen. Doctors found a chunk of metal—war's remains—covered with calcium.

They had several close calls, had seen enough horror to last a lifetime, and returned with a special reverence for life and rage to make up those lost months. Chuck tends to minimize any adjustment problems. He has quite erased them all. He found no hostility. "People in our town welcomed you with open arms." Then, on reflection, Chuck says, "The more I think back on it—the more I question how minimal my readjustment was." After the first six months, Chuck simply disappeared. He rented a little house in the wilderness and "just holed up there. I barely saw anybody for a year, except in my classes. I maybe had two, three dates in the whole year. It was the strangest thing, so out of character for someone like me. Then I woke up one morning and said, 'Okay, enough of this. It's time to get back to society.' It was my way to do it. I have tremendous sympathy and understanding for the veterans who seek help in the Vet

Centers today. I just happened to be more disciplined."

Tom, on the other hand, flew into emotional, crying rages. He slid into deep depressions, heavy drinking, and debilitating guilts "about all those people we slaughtered." The drinking was, in part, to stop the nightmares, but they came anyway. Some were recurring—in color. Even the smells, the burning fires, and the burning flesh returned in those dreams. And always the eyes.

Chuck thinks three things helped him adjust better than Tom. "I was a little older. At 19 and 21, that age difference is very important. Plus, I had some college and could rationalize all this a little better. And finally, like I said, it was easier just because of what I believed: If America was involved, then it's right. I'm a believer—always have been—in the idea that whatever cards you're dealt are the ones you've got to play with. And there's no point in whining. I went about trying to get my life in order and not reaching back into what happened. I don't have these same problems that Tom has about guilt and these emotional feelings."

In fact, the stories have been so long buried that there are, astonishingly, mutual moments that the Hagel brothers had not ever shared over the years. Tom is hearing, for the first time, in his brother's home, exactly how Chuck saved him 14 years before.

It was late in the afternoon and they were in the last of several APCs (Armored Personnel Carriers), lumbering steel–plated behemoths called "tracks." They were on their way back to an old Michelin rubber plantation after an unsuccessful search of a village. The enemy watched and, when it looked as if they could get the last track, they opened up. A command-detonated mine went off underneath Chuck and Tom's track with a horrendous blast. Chuck was soon in flames, his left side burning, his face a mass of bubbles. Both eardrums were broken by the blast. Tom was concussed and unconscious.

"I thought he was dead," recalls Chuck. "I started throwing everybody off the track. With all the ammunition we had, it would just blow. I grabbed Tom and he was just dead weight."

"Is that how I got out of there?" Tom interrupts.

Chuck tugged and threw Tom off, then landed on top of him, just before the VC opened up on them with machine guns. They were shielded in part by the huge burning track. GIs in the tracks up front heard the explosion and returned fast enough. "If they hadn't, it would have been all over. They would have either killed us or taken us prisoner."

It seemed like hours to Chuck before they got back to the rubber plantation. His scorched face was bubbled and blistered; the pain was nearly unbearable. When Tom woke up in the plantation, he groped around and immediately hollered to the medic for Chuck. "He's right here," said the medic, "in the bunk next to you."

A few years have passed since Myra McPherson interviewed Chuck Hagel for her book. But not much has changed. He is affable, well-spoken, and courteous. . . the all-American boy grown up.

Chuck still believes his involvement in Vietnam was the right thing to do. Originally, his orders were supposed to go to Germany during the war. He volunteered to go to Vietnam.

"I thought that it was important that we have our best people in Vietnam, and I felt that I could contribute something," he says.

Over the years, Chuck has not only been tremendously successful in his own career pursuits, he was also an integral supporter of Jan Scruggs' vision for the Vietnam Veterans Memorial.

"When I first heard about it [the Wall], I was the deputy administrator of the Veterans Administration in 1981. I was, at the time, the highest ranking combat Vietnam veteran in the Reagan administration," he explains. Because of his position, he got caught up in the middle of the controversy surrounding the Wall. "Those who were opposed to the Wall came to talk to me about it. They tried to bludgeon me to change my position. Essentially, I said we all have to remember, as Vietnam veterans, that our mission is to get a Memorial up to honor those who served and those who contributed. The form of that Memorial, in my opinion, was not all that important. I thought the process the Vietnam Veterans Memorial Fund had suggested and implemented was fair. The ground rules had been set, they were agreed to, so let's let that process work. And whatever comes out of it, comes out of it."

"My point was: Let's get a Memorial up, and let's move on with honoring those who served, MIAs, and POWs, and try and piece this country back together from that experience," he says.

Plans to build the Memorial progressed. In March 1982, the ground-breaking ceremony took place. Chuck was one of the speakers at the ceremony. "There were, I think, four or five of us who spoke, Senators Mathias and Warner and Governor Robb at the time, and me. Jan Scruggs was the MC and we were the main speakers. I'll never forget that day. It was a bitterly cold day. March 26th, I believe, 1982. And I thought, of course as anyone would, about a friend who didn't come back...and I thought about the experiences I had, and how you grow from that experience. There were a lot of flashbacks, a lot of currents of consciousness that streamed through. I also had complete admiration for the job that Jan and his people had done to make all this happen. It was quite a remarkable accomplishment. And I thought very, very appropriate for honoring those who served.

"I also thought, you know this was 1982, we were breaking ground and in a few months, by Veterans Day, it would be completed. It was less than 10 years since the last American troops had been pulled out of Vietnam, and yet we were now on the threshold of erecting a monument to those who served. That was just spectacular. Nothing happens that fast, especially in the context of a very unpopular divisive war.''

As the dedication ceremony approached, the public waited, unsure of what to think about the Memorial. ''There wasn't an immediate embrace of it,'' Chuck recalls. ''It was a strange thing, kind of an aberration. You know, nobody was really opposed to honoring the Vietnam veterans, but there was a 'wait and see' attitude. And it all started with the design. We had never seen a design like it. Nothing in Washington is quite like that. All of our Memorials are above ground. I think that the Memorial itself was one of those strange anomalies that grows on people. And there's a certain amount of mysticism that surrounds it. There's a mystical feeling about it. . . a different feeling about it. And how befitting. How appropriate for the most drawn out, misunderstood, debated conflict that this country has ever been involved in. . . how appropriate to have a Memorial like this. And it says different things to different people in different ways, but still captures the core, the essence of what I think most people remember about that conflict.

''And the press picked up on it. I think as people came to Washington to see it, it was just one of those things that's almost indescribable and undefinable. You have to see it and experience it and walk it and be there to really get the true sense of its power. That has come through over the years, so that now it's the most visited Memorial in Washington.''

Of the names on that Wall, Chuck knew as many as 16 or 20 personally. As buddies. And there were many, many more that he saw die, but didn't know well. ''You saw people killed all around you,'' he says. ''I was there in 1968, and on one occasion within two hours every officer was killed in our battalion, and most all our Sergeants were killed. In fact, I had been in the country two months, as a Private 1st Class, a PFC, and for one week I was the company Sergeant. They chose me to be the Sergeant for the company because everybody had been killed. Me. . .a Private with two months experience in Vietnam.''

Much is said regarding the healing nature of the Wall. As Chuck mentioned, ''healing'' means different things to different people. Chuck says, ''When I think of healing, the healing power of that Wall, I think first you deal with what's happened through kind of a mirrored process. If you've seen the Wall, you've seen how it kind of looks back at you and reflects. It helps a Vietnam veteran, I think, to step up to it and deal with it. You face it, you see the names and the mirror comes back at you. You see yourself among the names. It hits you directly, you don't escape, it's there. Secondly, it's comforting in how it kind of envelops you, the way those two walls come to a V, and then both walls kind of come around you. It's a warm feeling I get. It's a feeling that these names will be there forever. It says to me that they in fact did not die for nothing. It says to me that these people will be remembered. Where the Wall is, next to the Lincoln Memorial, also gives it a strong positive feeling. And with a healing, you move on. . . feeling a little better maybe about what's gone on in the past. . .and feeling better that the people who sacrificed so much won't be forgotten.''

Healing is a gradual process. Each time you visit the Wall, Chuck says, ''You get some new feelings, partly because you are more comfortable every time you're there. You're more comfortable with the situation, with your feelings, and with the Wall. Therefore, you allow more things to seep into your consciousness and your psyche. . .thoughts and feelings that weren't there the first time you went. And when you are more comfortable, you reach for it, maybe a little more than you did before, and sometimes it just comes over you."

During the first five years after the Wall was built, Chuck visited it often. He likes to spend time there. Any time he has guests come in from out of town, he plays tour guide. For friends who are veterans, he takes the lead from them as to whether they want to talk about the past while they walk the Wall. Some do. Many don't. It's still not an easy thing for many veterans to discuss. Chuck doesn't mind talking about it. But his brother Tom does. So he understands how different people, even those from the same family with similar experiences, choose to heal in their own ways.

And there's always the unexpected reactions many have to the Wall. Some are overcome. Many are awestruck. "I think, aesthetically, people were quite surprised. They were caught by the beauty of it, the simplicity of it, the naturalness of it. I think especially hit people who didn't know what to expect. I think, too, the sheer quiet seductive power of the black granite and that mirror image really shocks people. And there's the awesomeness of those names. Probably, when people go they don't think too much about it, and then all of a sudden it hits them."

Even those, like Chuck, who were close to the Wall from the start have been surprised by the effect the Wall has on people. "I guess the two things I've been struck by is the way people do the rubbings [of the names] ...and then the leaving of the mementos, which is like a catharsis. It's an act...a release...an action, that symbolizes something to them. And it has an effect on them that they might not get any other way. It's a symbolic feeling and gesture...it's essentially an expression of feelings."

The Wall also has an inherent ability to bring people together. To cause them to cross paths. To form bonds. And friendships. "One day, I was looking at the Wall,"

Chuck says. "And I was looking for a guy by the name of Saunders, he was a young kid who was killed when we were crossing a stream. I found his name and I saw another guy standing there with me. I didn't know what he was looking at. He didn't know what I was looking at. But in fact we were looking at Saunders' name. This guy had known Saunders in basic training. And he had gone to Vietnam with Saunders, but with different units. They were separated. He later found out that Saunders had been killed. So we started talking, and I said, 'Well I was right there at the time Saunders was killed.' "

Chuck is currently Chairman of the 10th Anniversary Commemoration Committee for the Vietnam Veterans Memorial. He hopes to hold a number of symposiums around the country at a dozen universities. Each would address various topics and bring back people who were part of that time as speakers. The goal is to reflect, and gain some historical perspective on that era. "Emotionally, in most cases," he says, "we're far enough away now to give a more honest perspective and analysis. We're not interested in replaying the debate, but rather to reflect on history." During that week of Veterans Day, a second candlelight vigil will be held for the reading of the names on the Wall. There will be commemorative events like addresses, wreath laying ceremonies, and reunions similar to those held 10 years ago for the dedication.

There will also be plans for the travelling Wall. For those who are unable to visit the nation's capital, a visit to the travelling Wall can be an equally important, and cherished, experience.

"I think probably the most important element of this 10-year celebration and reflection is 'inclusiveness.' We want to include people. We want to include organizations. And we want to include anybody who wants to part of this commemoration."

For veterans who have chosen not to visit the Wall,

perhaps out of fear or anger, Chuck has these words of encouragement. "I would tell them that they should consider going. Number one, because it's really sacred ground for them as a Vietnam veteran. They deserve to go. They deserve to place themselves in that environment . . . in that aura . . . enveloped by the names of those who served and died in Vietnam. They owe it to themselves to do that. Second, it's a beautiful peaceful place. I think they can find much comfort there personally. And lastly, whatever demons are still down inside them, many can be driven out with the experience of going to the Wall . . . taking some time just to be there."

CARMELLA LASPADA

In the late 1960s, Carmella LaSpada took a USO tour to Southeast Asia, as part of her job as a Special Projects Aide at the White House.

"That was the closest I ever came to war," she says. She remembers watching an endless stream of casualties coming in to the hospital. The battle of Dak To had just been fought. It was November 1967.

Carmella was asked to visit the men on the ward and spend as much time as possible with them, talking, listening, and holding their hands. While there, she spoke with one young medic. He told her that 35 of his buddies had died. With tears in his eyes, he described how they screamed out to him in pain. Frantically, he ran from one dying man to another. Praying. And crying. He tried everything he could to soothe their pain. But there were just too many who needed help. Much too many for one man to save.

As he told his story, he looked up and asked Carmella, "Will you promise me something?"

"Sure, whatever I can do. What is it?" she replied.

He explained that his battalion was known as the Black Scarf battalion, nicknamed after a big battle they had won against the Viet Cong. With the VC's black pajamas, they made themselves scarves that they wore around their necks. Slowly, he handed her his scarf. On it was a 1/2 symbol stitched in yellow. Carmella hesitated before taking it. She knew it meant so much to this young man.

"I really want you to have it," he said. "I want you to remember them and maybe you'll be able to do something so that those men—my buddies—who died, and their families, will never be forgotten."

And so Carmella made a promise. It was a promise

she never broke. It was a promise that forever changed her life.

"I never knew what happened to him," Carmella says. "He was 19 . . . and the sweetest guy. He had blond hair. I think his name was John."

When Carmella returned to the states she set out to do whatever she could to fulfill her promise. Always, she kept thinking how important it was for this young man—and all the others she had met—that something be done for the ones who lost their lives in battle.

Through her work at Walter Reed, she learned more and more about POWs and MIAs. Many of the men she met at the hospital told her stories of friends who were missing or imprisoned. Then, she began to hear that many of these same men had families. At that point, there were nearly 2,500 children of POWs and MIAs.

It was July 1971. Carmella decided that for the next six months she'd work on doing something for these kids. Then, by January she'd start cultivating her career in broadcasting.

For her first project, Carmella rallied together sports figures and toy manufacturers. In a massive effort to play Santa Claus, Carmella and her few supporters collected toys, gifts, autographs, and letters to send to the kids whose fathers would not be sharing Christmas with them. In only two weeks—on a shoestring budget—Carmella sent out roughly 4,000 gifts to kids.

"And that was going to be it," she says with a laugh. "But then the calls started coming in and so did the letters. One of the first calls was this mother who said, 'You cannot imagine what this meant to my youngster.' She said, 'A month ago, he came home crying one day from school. He was six years old.' He said 'Mommy, Mommy, Daddy isn't a murderer is he?' 'But the gifts, the letters, and the autographed photos from you—I've never seen such a change in him.'"

Carmella began to realize that she was helping these

children develop a sense of self-esteem—at a time when they needed it most—during the formative years. She was impacting how the children felt about themselves, their father and their country. So, she set out to do a little more—but only for six more months. Then, she'd focus on broadcasting.

Six more months came and went. Now it's 20 years later, and Carmella is still active in helping the children of veterans. She has also begun helping children whose parents are victims of terrorism, like the hostages.

Out of her efforts, *No Greater Love* was formed. Through *No Greater Love*, children of veterans were remembered through cards, gifts and letters on the days and moments that meant the most to them—birthdays, Father's Day, holidays. At its peak, *No Greater Love* sent out 15,000 gifts to children.

Throughout the 1970s, *No Greater Love* continued to reach out to more and more children. They established special children's ceremonies for Memorial Day and Veterans Day. All the while, Carmella knew that what was needed was a monument or Memorial that could be a central place for these children to pay their respects to their fathers. She also knew she would not be the right person to push for such an idea. After all, she was a civilian. And a woman. In her prayers, she hoped that someone would someday build a Memorial to these men.

Just as she was beginning to feel America no longer needed an organization like *No Greater Love* (because the children of Vietnam vets were now all grown up) the Iran hostage crisis broke. And then came Beirut. There was still a need for *No Greater Love*.

It was about that same time Jan Scruggs visited Carmella and told her of his idea. She remembers that visit. "He was an answer to my prayers. He was the man that could do this."

As the dedication ceremonies for the Vietnam

Veterans Memorial approached, Carmella asked Jan if the children could participate in the events and be the first ones to place a wreath at the Wall. He agreed it would be a great idea.

On the day the Wall was dedicated, a handful of children, escorted by a Vietnam veteran who had received the Medal of Honor, placed the first wreath near the center of the Wall. For the children, the Wall represents a promise that their fathers will always be remembered.

"What is so important about the Wall is that it's a tangible symbol—something physical—that shows these children that their father's name never will be forgotten," she explains. "*No Greater Love* is an expression of love through actions. It's our 'living Memorial' to each father. The Wall is that same reflection in a physical symbol. Both parts really make it complete for the kids."

After the children placed the wreath at the Wall, they also lovingly placed roses beside each panel. One hundred and forty-four roses were left that day. This meant so much to the children involved that on the 10th anniversary of the fall of Saigon, April 30, 1985, they asked Carmella if another similar ceremony could be performed. Again, a wreath was laid at the Wall and roses left behind.

When Carmella started to realize how important these small gestures were to the children, she organized a special Father's Day program. She contacted children across the country and offered to deliver any child's personal message—a note, a letter, or card—to the Wall on Father's Day. The response was tremendous. On Father's Day that year, Carmella and a small crowd of sons and daughters delivered bags of cards and letters to the Wall. Beside the notes of love, they also left a bouquet of fresh flowers.

Carmella has visited the Wall with many children, often taking them there for the very first time. She describes the feeling the children experience. "It's something very personal. Beyond words. It's something that speaks from the heart . . . they are so taken by the sheer emotion of being there. They feel sad . . . and yet there is an uplifting feeling in knowing their father is remembered. It makes them feel they didn't die in vain."

She remembers one time recently when one of the volunteers at *No Greater Love*, a Vietnam veteran named Tom, escorted a young man to the Wall to see his father's name. The son, part of the 82nd Airborne in Desert Storm, was four years old when his father received a Medal of Honor posthumously. Tom took the boy to the Wall in the early morning hours to avoid the crowds.

"It was just the best time for them to go," she says. "It really worked out well, and it meant so much to him because he never knew his father."

Regardless of the time, day or night, there are people at the Wall. Carmella has also visited the Wall at all hours. She says, "You can go in the morning . . . in the evening . . . even at dawn, and see people. You can tell the tourists, and you can tell the families of veterans . . . or people who knew them. You almost feel their pain when you see them weeping. Night is my favorite time to visit. Of course, you can't see the names, but there's such a stillness—and darkness—that it emphasizes the tragedy of war. At night as you walk from one end to the other, the walk seems almost endless, because the dark makes it hard to see where the Wall ends."

Carmella describes the sensitivity it takes to escort a new visitor to the Wall. "When they go there, it's best to escort them there, then walk away and let them express their own feelings alone in their own private way. Grief is so different with so many people. I think they feel a loss, but they feel a love."

It's not just the children who are moved by their visits to the Wall. Carmella, too, has strong feelings. She says, "When you first see it, you see the black marble and you notice it's down in the ground, not like other Memorials...and you look at it, and remember that Vietnam was called the black hole of the soul. I feel that it's incredible how it touches people...and the way it mirrors you when you walk with the names. It's the type of Memorial that says it all."

Carmella also reflects on the past when she visits the Wall. "I often wonder how many of those names [of the men from the hospital] are up there. I visited a couple of thousand men in those 10 days. When I look at it and remember them, it [the Wall] says pain and suffering. I look at that Wall and I think of the families that they left behind. The Wall kind of grows on you, it did with me. It really did and the more I thought about it, the more I realized each time I go it becomes more powerful to me."

"You always remember the dead," she says. "The Wall allowed a unity to take place. It's about the dead and the living coming together."

SHAUN SHEEHAN

The City of Angels slept, unaware that a few miles away LAX airport bustled with activity as hundreds of duffle bags, helmets, canteens, love notes, and young soldiers were bused to waiting planes. Baritone voices barked orders into the cool midnight air. Nearly eight planes a night left carrying soldiers to Vietnam. Departures were staged in the middle of the night so that civilians didn't see the scores of troops leaving. The year was 1968, towards the end of the Tet Offensive. The buildup of troops continued, though it seemed more like a war of attrition.

Shaun Sheehan, a graduate of the Marine Corps Officer Candidate's School, was among those rushed to Northern I Corps. "The strategy at that time was to attempt to engage the North Vietnamese mainline units in 'search and destroy' types of operations with a battalion or larger. It was an attempt to draw them out and let our superior fire power blow them to death. And we did a lot of dying in the process," Shaun says. From March through July that year, Shaun's main responsibility was to coordinate artillery strikes to support a rifle company of roughly 150 marines in the field.

During that period, he went out on three separate major engagements, or operations. "We went out with approximately 150 guys," he recalls, "and each time, came back with less than 40." Not every one of them was killed. Many were wounded. Others were disabled by malaria, massive dehydration, and infection. "Nothing healed. . . because there was so much infection in that environment and it was a semi-tropical climate. For instance, you could get a flesh wound—maybe cut yourself in your kitchen right now—and with a Band-Aid and a little Mercurochrome it's going to heal up. Well [in Vietnam] it wouldn't heal up."

On one of the missions Shaun went out on, his unit was overrun in the middle of the night by the enemy. "They were in the middle of us, they were from me to you," he says gesturing towards me. "And that's scary. I think on reflection that was probably the scariest moment. A lot of kids got killed."

He remembers the terrain of Vietnam as if it lies just beyond his fourth floor office window. "There were two basic types of landscape. One was elephant grass and rice paddies. . . flat. Then mountains rising straight up with a triple canopy of trees—you know one set of trees, then another and a third. So, I was either in the mountains, where you would wake up above the clouds a lot of times. . . or down in elephant grass that could be higher than your waist, sometimes up to your chest. Your arms would be just a mass of cuts. But you had to keep cutting through the grass to get anywhere. You couldn't get your breath. The big problem of cutting— the manual labor—is simply that there was no air."

His memories of combat are just as vivid. "I distinctly recall one of the weapons they [the North Vietnamese] employed against us were anti-aircraft guns that were lowered and were shooting point blank at us. So I'm not talking about walking around in the middle of woods looking for some little guy with a rusty rifle. I'm talking about the real McCoy," he says.

"I was the only guy on my team that didn't get shot. I recall running across the field one day, and because my helmet didn't fit—none of the American helmets really fit right—so my head was kind of down as I was running, and I could see bullets going between my legs," he says.

"The Vietnamese buried above the ground. So they'd make these mounds, and we'd go behind the mound because it provided perfect protection. The radio operator kept saying, 'Lieutenant, they're shooting at me.' And I yelled, 'They're shooting at all of us. Just shut up, and do your job.' So when we stopped that night, that kid showed me that he had his antenna shot off; he had bullets buried in his radio; he had three bullet holes in the swing of his rifle; and a shot hit his canteen. I just looked at him and said, 'You're right, they are shooting at you.' We just laughed.... there's a guileless humor to it."

"We actually had so many casualties that I got promoted back to an artillery battery," he says ironically. "That was still a forward unit, but compared to going out into the mountains like that, I felt I was going to Beverly Hills."

There is always pride in a job well done. Even in war. "My proudest moment was towards the end of my tour, with maybe a month to go," Shaun remembers. "The Colonel came out to our hill and took me aside. He prefaced his remarks by stating that a simple 'No' was all he needed to hear. Then, he asked me to extend my tour, to stay in Vietnam, and accept a senior position— to take over a unit. I said, 'Look, I'm a three-year Marine, always have been, so I'm out of here.' But it's a very flattering thing, believe it or not, to be asked. And he didn't pressure me."

For one particular job well done, Shaun was decorated for individual action. "I put up a big antenna when we were setting up, and they zeroed their mortars on where we were. Mortar fire was just raining down. So I crawled out of there, directed and counted battery fire—which I was supposed to be doing anyway—and got lucky and wiped them out. That resulted in all kinds of secondary explosions," he says with a slight pause. "I didn't scour until after the action. That's when I realized my radio operator had been killed. And another guy had been severely wounded. It makes it difficult to reflect on your individual success, expertise, and ability to perform under pressure, when you recognize that a youngster who was very close to you is gone. He [the soldier] had been accepted in the police academy, and he was going to go home in a couple of months. His whole life was in front of him." Receiving recognition for a mission in which a friend was killed was, at the very least, bittersweet. Even today, there's a sense he still carries the guilt.

Shaun left Vietnam in March 1969 and became the company commander of a recruit company. He viewed his mission simply: to finish out the six months left before he was sent home. "But then I saw how green [inexperienced] these kids were and realized that they could be the replacements for the kids I was with. It's always the green replacement kids you worried about the most because although they are trained and everything, they still haven't ever been shot at." So, Shaun became much harder. . . stricter. . . less forgiving of the boys. It was an effort to try to toughen them up before they saw combat. "That's really how the mystique of the Marine Corps carries on," he explains.

Combat isn't the only disaster these boys had to be prepared for. There were plenty of casualties sustained by friendly fire.

"Friendly fire happens," Shaun says. "It has always happened. Because there's immense fire power. I saw Marines killed by friendly fire from everything from a .45 to a B-52. I had a 1st Sergeant who had been at Iwo Jima, got out of the Marine Corps for 10 years, and came back in for Vietnam. He was killed by our Air Force, sitting at a desk. I remember watching this one truck, with about 12 Marines on it, blow up when a kid threw his flak jacket up into the truck and pulled the pin on a grenade. It blew up him and everybody in the truck. They consider that friendly fire, too. If you are going to engage in close range, friendly fire occurs, and it occurs a lot. Especially if our core tactic is massive fire power— which it was in Vietnam. With Desert Storm, there was a lot of disgust over friendly fire. I watched the press reports, they couldn't understand. But I understood."

In November 1969, Shaun came home. No longer an active Marine, perhaps always a Marine at heart. Now it was time to assimilate back into society. To carry on. "You try and put everything behind you, and you can't," he says. "When you get home, you have tremendous guilt. Your guilt centers on the fact that you got home. And you left a lot of friends. It's very difficult to deal with that."

At the time, most of Shaun's friends were in graduate school. The anti-war movement was in full-swing. But Shaun was exhausted. Too tired to pick a side. Too numb to take part in the intellectual debates that waged on in living rooms and dining rooms, on campuses and TV.

"I was not only a veteran, but truly a combat veteran. I mean, you are so exhausted mentally and physically. Besides, you see both sides of things. It wasn't black and white for somebody like me, it was tremendously gray," he explains. Yet for most of the graduate students he knew it was all one way...and for most adults that remembered World War II, it was the other way. "I was just happy to be alone, I really liked being left alone," he says. "Time really brings you out of it, but you feel guilty. And that's what needed healing."

"When I first came back, God I forgot about this," he says shaking his head, "I'd be driving a car, and sometimes I'd pull over when cars were coming at me. I mean you've got an instrument there, that if someone wants to steer at you, they could. And you couldn't walk in a room that I was in at night, where I wouldn't wake up. You couldn't come down the hall without me waking up."

Shortly after arriving home, Shaun went to Europe for a year. Then returned home and settled into the work force. He nurtured a career in broadcasting and became Senior Vice President of the National Association of

Broadcasters—the lobby representing the radio and television industry.

While there, he received a call from Bill Jayne. Bill was working with Jan Scruggs to erect the Vietnam Veterans Memorial. When they heard Shaun was a veteran—with ties to the media—they contacted him to see if he was interested in supporting their efforts. At first he was a bit skeptical.

He remembers saying, "Why don't you just get them some decent benefits and call it a day? What are you building a Memorial for?" Jayne asked him to at least listen to their proposal. Shaun agreed. He attended a gathering where Jan Scruggs spoke, simply and eloquently, about the need to recognize the millions of kids who participated—and lost their lives—in an episode so critical to our nation's fabric. That recognition should take the form of a Memorial. He also stressed the importance of having a Memorial that did not make a political statement.

"I'm kind of a history buff. So, that made an awful lot of sense to me. Because at that point in time, Vietnam was being forgotten, just swept under the rug," says Shaun. "I had direct access to the networks and all the radio and television stations. I also had the ability to facilitate an awareness campaign, so I kind of took that on. I think we were very, very successful."

In retrospect, Shaun says, "The thing that helped the Memorial is the fact that the American embassy personnel were taken hostage in Iran. I think the United States became upset at the treatment of its victims, its international victims. For some reason this rekindled a latent national guilt over the way the Vietnam veteran had been treated. I think it spurred our fund raising campaign. Sometimes, that fact and those events get glossed over."

"We were very, very successful in creating national awareness. And we were very successful in raising money.

We ended up succeeding despite ourselves, which of course is the great part . . . that is the wonderful part of the story."

From the beginning, Shaun was enthralled by Maya Lin's design. He spent many long, arduous hours defending it against the "right wing element that felt it was an anti-war statement."

"I wasn't concerned so much with the aesthetics, my point was we really needed this as a national reminder," he says.

Because he was a critical element in the project's success, he was asked to take part in the ground-breaking ceremonies. "Initially when I was asked to be a ground-breaker, my thinking was to decline. I just didn't want to." Shaun didn't want to take advantage of having been blessed while in combat. Memories of that young radio operator still plagued him. He dared not profit in any way from his experiences while others had lost so much.

"I think in our memories we become more valiant every year. The fact of the matter is, we were scared kids. The tough part is some of your friends, you know, never had kids. That's the tough part. Then I thought about the fact that I had two little boys. I thought it would be special for them to have the opportunity to be there," he says. "Really, in the end, I was honored and gratified just to be asked."

As a national reminder, Shaun believes the Wall "succeeded beyond anything ever imagined. There is power—a sort of healing power—in walking down there and just looking at those names. It's very powerful and very difficult for a lot of guys to go there. I have many friends who still can't get themselves to go. Never. But in some kind of a dark sense, they are proud that it's there." The fact that the Wall is there—should they ever find the desire to go—is what matters. Its mere existence speaks loudly.

Shaun, like many other veterans, fears that the

perception of Vietnam veterans is an incorrect one. Yes, there are scars—both mental and physical—that haunt many veterans today. But haunting is quite different from debilitating.

"I think it's important for people, like me, to come forward. People who are in the upper echelon, the ones America has been very good to. Because not everybody that went to Vietnam walks around in khakis or a camouflage outfit, mourning what happened 25 years ago. A hell of a lot of us have gotten on with our lives," he explains. "We have ascended in the leadership functions of society—which is only appropriate. I'm 48 years old. It's time. It's where my generation ought to be."

"I empathize with those who need treatment," he continues, "but I think there was a fixation at one point in time—especially among the industry I work for, the media—to categorize the Vietnam veteran as some dysfunctional guy in a combat outfit . . . who can't hold a job . . . and has a drug problem. Now we've got a Medal of Honor recipient running for President of the United States, who seems in his politics to be more liberal and skeptical of the military. On the other hand, we've got a United States Senator from Arizona who was a POW for six-plus years, who stays more to the right and is pro-military. Those guys wear suits and ties to go to work. So I think the myth of the dysfunctional veteran is exploding and deservedly so."

In many instances, Vietnam made men like Shaun keener. More adept. "At first, you lost ground to the people that went to graduate school and got the good jobs to start. It took people, like me, four or five years to regain confidence in themselves. You don't recognize it at the time, but the experience of performing under a true crisis environment gives you the ability to function in other types of crises. That really can't be taught in school. It gives you an advantage. You have the ability to weigh what's important and what isn't important. You don't get scared. And you're normally prepared," he says.

As for the Wall, he says, "I've never been a touchy, feely kind of guy. But the thing that kind of overwhelms me has been the success of the Memorial. I suspect over time that will dwindle. But the fact of the matter is it's there and it's a physical testament to what occurred. And I think it correctly honors those who gave the most, and I think you take from it what you want to take from it."

"Desert Storm kind of brought things full cycle for me. I subsequently found out that I've got three friends who were regimental commanders in Marine combat units, who were little 1st and 2nd Lieutenants with me. I mean I had a pit in my stomach the day that the cruise missiles first started. And it really gnawed at me because I knew what the kids would be going through. I am very gratified, as others are, that the casualties that they sustained were so light," he says. Today, Shaun still has the same feelings about the Wall that he did more than 10 years ago. From the first time he looked at the pastel sketch of the design, "I just kind of liked it. It was simple." Shaun visits the Memorial a couple of times a year. "I drive by quite often. I'm always amazed by the crowds. I never expected it," he says in wonderment. Perhaps because he knows "Vietnam wasn't World War II. To this moment we don't know relative right or wrong." And yet, there is nothing more "right" than the Wall.

LOOKING BACK

Shaun Sheehan was intimately involved in the efforts to build the Vietnam Veterans Memorial. In the spring of 1983, he was asked by then-VVMF Chairman of the Board, John Wheeler, to submit a personal reflection on the monument. Here are the words he wrote on April 7, 1983:

I rather thought that I had gotten on with life and that Vietnam, which of course would always be a pivotal event in my experience, had recessed into the appropriate corner of my psyche. Suffice to say an emotion I really felt had dissipated surfaced. Further, I knew that professionally I was in a position to help both through this industry [the media] and with the Fund in aiding the structuring of their outreach efforts.

I was drawn to the approach being taken, namely the skirting of a political statement and the singular drive to erect a national monument. In my opinion, future historians will fashion the true definition of what Vietnam was; present society through this drive was creating the recognition within the population that indeed Vietnam occurred and that the structure itself would embody this acknowledgement thereby creating the living testament that cannot be ignored now or in the future.

As the design controversy erupted, I was first concerned that this would hamper fundraising and then as the situation became more tense there certainly was the possibility of the project being jeopardized. The speed with which all was accomplished and the obstacles met is truly amazing. Moreover, the staff itself was amateur, it gained expertise as it progressed. The real progress never ceased to amaze me.

When the invitation was extended to participate in the

ground-breaking my initial reaction was to decline out of a strange sense that Vietnam, in many ways, was good to me. I have my health and some degree of prosperity and on the whole it could be argued that I profited by the experience. I had a similar reaction when I rotated home in March 1969. It is a simple guilt for being whole while so many weren't. I understand it is a quite common reaction but still quite startling to experience personally.

Obviously, I am glad I did participate in the ceremony. It will remain a memorable date both for myself and my family.

When the question regarding placement of the flag and the statue erupted, I attempted to try and see the opposition's position. I walked the monument grounds one day, which reconfirmed my belief that the initially selected design was valid, but that if additional elements were to be added, that the Fund's recommendation was correct. I remember walking to the Lincoln Memorial and rereading the Gettysburg Address in which Lincoln eloquently stated that words would never suffice nor replace the actions that had occurred. It made me think about the negative reaction by some to the Memorial mirroring the debate that remains on the very subject of Vietnam and I found a correlation between what Lincoln's reaction was and the present situation. I felt a certain irony.

BARBARA SONNEBORN

Widow of Jeff Gurvitz

On February 28, 1968, Barbara Gurvitz was driving home from work. It was late afternoon on a cold, wintery Chicago day. Suddenly, she was seized by sharp, shooting pains in her stomach.

She remembers, "I literally had to pull the car over to the side and pant. I thought that I was getting a stomach flu or something—like appendicitis. I didn't know what it was. But I felt horribly sick to my stomach. The pain passed in about 10–15 minutes."

Years later, while reviewing some military documents, Barbara confirmed the afternoon she was stricken with pain was also the morning her husband, Jeff Gurvitz, was killed in Vietnam. It was February 29, 1968.

Jeff died during a mortar attack. He crawled out of a foxhole to rescue his wounded radio operator. Just then, another mortar hit. It hit too quickly. There was nowhere to go. Jeff was killed by multiple metal fragment wounds, as was his radio operator. It killed them and four others. In that particular action six men were killed and some 25 more were injured.

"Ironically," Barbara says, "part of why I loved him was because he was that kind of a person. . . the kind of person who, if he saw a burning car and someone had to be rescued—and everyone was standing around screaming—he would have dove in to rescue the person even though the car might explode."

Barbara remembers how she found out about her husband's death. "It was March 2, 1968. My 24th birthday. I was awakened that morning by the doorbell ringing. I thought I was alone in the house—my parents had gone out shopping. I was going to have lunch with some friends for my birthday. I got up and went to the door and asked, 'Who is it?' Someone called through [the door] 'United States Army.' I opened the door and there was this man with a long face, and he said, 'I regret to inform you that your husband is missing in action in Vietnam.'"

Barbara's knees buckled. This had to be a bad dream.

Barbara and Jeff were childhood sweethearts. He was a handsome boy with dark hair, and big, beautiful brown eyes framed by long, lush lashes. He had a dynamic, magnetic personality. "A natural born leader," they'd say. After high school, they attended the University of Illinois in Champaign/Urbana together.

Jeff joined the Army ROTC program in college, with hopes of going on to law school. ROTC seemed the best way for Jeff, whose family had little money, to get an education.

On August 22, 1965, a few months after they graduated, Barbara and Jeff married. That fall, she attended graduate school at the University of Chicago, and he started law school.

"He had very ambivalent feelings about law school. It's what he was expected to do but not what he really wanted to do," Barbara says. "He knew he had to get this Army obligation out of the way."

By 1965, the Vietnam War had already begun. Barbara and Jeff argued over whether he should quit school and enter the Army to fulfill his obligation. Another year passed. And the war waged on. Jeff began to feel more strongly about his need to enlist. Against everybody's wishes—except his father's—Jeff joined the Army in early 1967.

"I was opposed to the war by then. He didn't know what to feel. He didn't know why we were there [in Vietnam]. But he felt he had signed up for something and had an obligation to fulfill. He was a man of his own mind," Barbara remembers.

"At first, we fought about it. And really had some big arguments. But then it was clear that he had made up his mind. We just decided to stop fighting—and talking—about the politics of the war. I did not have the strength of my convictions to stand in his way. . .the way I would now,'' she says.

After basic training, Jeff had some choices as to where to go next. One option was Fort Ord, California.

"We were very excited about that possibility. We didn't know that Fort Ord was the direct route for the Army to go off to Vietnam. Not very long after we got out there, we realized the people he had come out with and those who had come shortly before him were getting orders for Vietnam," Barbara says.

In September 1967, Jeff received his orders. He was to leave for Vietnam on January 1st—New Year's Day—1968.

"We went out to California 10 days before he left so that we would have some time alone. We spent some days in Palm Springs and then about five days in San Francisco just pretending we were on vacation. But we were on vacation with very heavy hearts," says Barbara.

That was the last vacation Barbara and Jeff shared together.

Barbara recalls, "I had a fantasy of getting into an automobile accident right before he left, just a small one, I didn't want to get killed. I contemplated shooting him in the foot. He had taught me how to shoot a gun, and I thought, 'If I shoot him in the foot, he won't be able to wear a boot.' After he died, I struggled for a long time with guilt about not preventing him from going."

Barbara's guilt was likely compounded by the fact that her husband had in some odd way hinted at his fate.

"When we were young sweethearts, like 16–17 years old, he had said from the time I remember, 'I know I'm not going to live to be very old,'" she remembers. "He told my father he was sure he was not going to come back. But he did not tell that to me.

"From the time we heard that he was going to

Vietnam until the day that he died, I lived with a feeling that I had pincers in my heart."

Then, as the Army officer stood before her that March day in 1968—just two short months after her husband had left—those pincers shackled her heart with such grief and despair she could not escape it for years.

Barbara describes her reaction to the news. "The world just exploded around me. I really just kind of collapsed. I can't really remember any daylight. I remember that period of time as all night. I'm sure there were days, but I can't remember them. I just remember nights."

She continues, "I couldn't stand to be alone. There was always somebody with me. I cried a lot. I didn't eat hardly at all for a month. I lost 25 pounds. They were going to put me in the hospital. Then, I ate a little bit of applesauce. Because Jeff was killed by multiple metal fragment wounds, that was such powerful imagery to me that I couldn't stand to look at meat.

"I did go on with my life, but I had nightmares for about eight years. I had periods of nightmares and claustrophobia. Early in the '70s, which was four years after his death, I went through a period where I thought I was totally losing my mind. I couldn't be in dark spaces. I would go running out of movie theaters and elevators. I'd feel dizzy in dark places. I really thought I was losing my mind," she says. Through therapy and the support of family and friends, Barbara began to piece her life back together and try to let go of some of her grief.

By the late 1970s, there were rumblings that a Memorial might be built for the Vietnam veterans. Barbara recalls her reaction when she first heard about the Memorial. "After Jeff was killed, I didn't want to have anything to do with the military. I didn't want to hear about the military. I never used the commissary, the medical stuff. You mentioned anything 'official' about the Vietnam War and I didn't want to know about it.

I didn't go see the movies. I didn't look at television specials. And I didn't read any of the books."

She continues, "It wasn't that I was pretending it didn't happen, I just felt that I had my own imagery and I didn't need anymore. I felt sorry for the veterans that came back and were treated so badly. When I heard that there was going to be a Memorial, I thought it was a great idea, but I felt separated from that. I felt that my relationship with Jeff and his death was a private affair."

As news of the Memorial began to spread, Barbara's father kept close tabs on the progress Jan Scruggs and his supporters were making. He would give Barbara updates, but she was uninterested. Much of her uninterest was a result of her naivete, she explains. "I didn't attach Jeff to it. I felt so angry at the country that I didn't think they could make up for it with a Memorial. I didn't realize that this Memorial was not about the government, but rather that it was a private force making it happen. I had no vision of the profound importance of it at that early stage."

After the Wall was dedicated in November 1982, news of its unanticipated impact on visitors spread across the country.

"When I began hearing about the incredible impact that it had on the people who visited it, it began to sink in that this was no ordinary Memorial. . .that it had a life of its own and was an amazing healing force. I began reading a little bit about people who went there and the impact it had on them. Then my friend Wanda went and saw it. She was one friend who was a widow also. She said she just couldn't stop crying."

Barbara was still somewhat apprehensive about visiting. Throughout the mid-1980s, she made several trips to the East Coast from her California home, but never made it a point to stop in Washington.

She explains, "I was afraid to go see it. I think I was protecting myself from the amount of emotion that I thought it might bring up for me, I'm not sure. I still felt that Jeff's death was in my own private world. It didn't feel like he was part of the Memorial.''

Then, in 1986, a scaled-down replica of the Wall was created as a travelling Memorial. It was a way people across the country could be a part of the Wall without needing to travel to Washington.

''It was here in Fremont [California],'' Barbara says. ''I really had mixed feelings about going to see it. My parents went to see it and my mother said, 'You really have to go see this.' I think I just didn't want to see his name on there. But she said, 'Go.' So, I thought, 'Okay, I'll go.'''

''We went down there at night, around sunset, it was spring or summer. It turned out the night we went there was a Veterans Memorial ceremony. I thought, 'Oh no, I don't want to be in the middle of this.' And as we stood there, different men got up to tell their stories. One man said that he came and saw the names of 25 or 28 men who were killed on the same day he survived. And he started to cry. He talked about how much it meant to him that their names were on this Memorial.'' Barbara pauses and then says softly, ''Suddenly, I got it. The gravity of what this meant as a healing force came to me. I was really glad that I had come down to see it.

''We spent quite a lot of time there that night. We lit a candle for Jeff, and we lit a candle for my friend Wanda's husband. It gave me chills to realize—first of all—the number of names on the Wall. I knew how many men had been killed but seeing all those names still makes me dizzy.''

By the late 1980s, Barbara had begun working on a documentary about Vietnam widows. The film, titled ''Regret to Inform,'' grew out of a letter she wrote Jeff on the 20th anniversary of his death. Her research efforts for the project led her to Washington and to her first visit to the ''real'' Wall.

She describes her first trip. "The way it's designed, you're kind of looking around for it. Then suddenly it's just there. I went to the kiosk and found Jeff's name, which is on panel 42 E. I had to walk all along the Wall to get to that panel because I had come around the other side. And I remember my heart pounding in anticipation of seeing his name. I almost felt, I think, that I wanted his name not to be there. . . like it was a mistake. . . and he could be somewhere else. But it was there. And, you know, the power of walking along that Wall was like swimming through a sea of dead bodies. In a way, I mean it isn't really, there's no blood, but I get that sense. It's like a giant black granite bird crashed into the ground. The fact that it is at the level of the earth, I sort of have this vision that behind the Wall are the souls of the men who are on it.

"I was just kind of struck dumb by its power," Barbara says. "I stood and looked at Jeff's name for a long time. I felt a certain kind of closure. . . that this was a very right thing. . . something as monumental as this, seemed like it belonged there."

Often, veterans, widows, and family members of those killed in action meet others at the Wall who have grieved as they have. Almost immediately, there is an unspoken bond as they meet. They can look in each other's eyes and say, "I know." Barbara, too, was one of thousands who have met by sharing their very personal and private moments together.

She describes that moment. "Because the weather was not very nice that day there weren't many people there. A woman came over to me and she asked, 'Who did you lose?' Obviously, it was clear to her that I was relating to the Wall, not just like a curiosity seeker. I said, 'My husband was killed.' And she asked, 'When?' I told her and said, 'What about you?' She looked clearly upset. She said, 'Well my husband's name should be on this Wall.' And I waited for her to go on. She said, 'He committed suicide three months ago. He just couldn't stand the flashbacks any longer.' She was so upset. We talked for a long time. She was the only person there that I had a conversation with. But at that moment, I realized that this is also a Memorial to the men whose names aren't on it.''

One of the most powerful aspects of the Wall is its ability to function on so many levels for so many different people—it allows the dead to be remembered, the living to grieve, strangers to embrace, and wounds to heal. For widows like Barbara, the Wall acknowledged their pain publicly and in a very real sense told them that after all the years of suppressed feelings, ''It's okay to feel the hurt you feel.''

''In America,'' Barbara explains, ''people mourn for a little while—a year at the most—and then you are supposed to be all better and put it behind you. It really doesn't work like that. With the Wall, there was suddenly this tremendous gesture of such profound respect and love for the men who died. And the process of people coming there and seeing the name of their loved one, then seeing somebody else there who shared the same thing makes people realize that they are not so alone.''

She adds, ''I don't think in the world there could be a more amazing Memorial than this Memorial. There's tremendous power in names. In ancient cultures when people died in battle they read the names at different ceremonies. . . and the passing down of names through generations has always been important. Now, these men who died in Vietnam are suddenly seen on this glorious piece of art. Now never forgotten.''

CAPTAIN KENNETH COSKEY

Tough as nails. That's the cliche that comes to mind when you talk with Captain Ken Coskey. How else to describe the person who survives four and a half years imprisonment as a POW—16 months spent in solitary confinement—and comes out relatively unscathed (except of course, for the small scars on his elbow and the annoying way his arm won't straighten enough for him to play golf)?

In 1968, Captain Coskey was a Navy commander stationed aboard the USS America. He was flying missions in accordance with President Johnson's bombing policy. One balmy night in September, his A-6 Intruder aircraft was shot down by a 35 mm shell over North Vietnam. He called it a "lucky shot."

The plane's engines died. All control was lost. Both the bombardier and Coskey ejected. As they did, the muggy air enveloped them like a cocoon. It was far from the crisp, air-conditioned coolness they'd left behind in the cockpit. The plane lit up the sky like a bright ball of fire. For a few moments, Coskey was mesmerized as he watch his plane go in. "As bright as it was, I figured everyone on the ground could see me," he told the *Opelika-Auburn News* in 1973. Those few moments were enough time to distract him from his landing strategy. He hit the ground stiff-legged, shattering his knee cap.

Once on the ground, he quickly discarded the survival gear clinging to his flight suit. He radioed the rescue helicopter "Clementine" for help. They were already on their way. Coskey felt confident he'd be rescued. After all, he had been hit only 10 miles from sea.

At that moment, Coskey looked up. Six Vietnamese soldiers had spotted him. At point-blank range, one fired a shot. It hit him in the elbow. He winced in pain as his captors surrounded him.

Then they made him walk. With each step, shooting pains from his wounded knee gripped his leg. His arm throbbed.

Here, Coskey remembers his days in captivity, in an article by Brad Ashmore, featured in the *Opelika-Auburn News*, shortly after Coskey returned home in 1973.

"We (Coskey and his captors) marched through several small villages and as I passed, the villagers grew more and more hostile. They kicked me, shoved, pushed, and spat on me. I was concerned that the guards might lose control and the mob would beat me to death. But the guards began clicking their rifle bolts at the mob and I made it through the crowd.

"Finally, the guards threw me on a truck because I couldn't walk any more. It was a terrible ride, the road was badly cratered by the bombs we had been dropping."

Captain Coskey was immediately interrogated by an English-speaking Vietnamese following his capture. That's when the beatings began.

"My captor's name was Tanh Shun Hoi and he took part in the beatings that first night after he shot me. At first, I gave them only my name, rank, date of birth, and serial number. I was forced to kneel on my broken knee cap with my arms tied behind me. My arm was really hurting me, so they pulled on it.

"I refused to answer their questions and they began to beat me with bamboo clubs. . .baseball type blows to the back of my legs and buttocks.

"I began to tell them lies and half-truths to stop the beatings, but it was just a cat-and-mouse game. I never told them anything that would help them or be critical to our pilots."

Coskey was taken to the home of his captor to await transport to Hanoi.

"I was placed in leg irons at night. They were so tight that I could not sleep, but they took the irons off in the daytime and I slept then. Tanh Shun Hoi's family, a grandmother, his wife, and daughter used sticks to keep me awake during the day.

"Later, they produced a picture of Ho Chi Minh. I spoke his name and they thought it was fantastic that I knew their leader. They marched me back to the road to be transported to Hanoi a few days later and there I was placed on a truck with then-Colonel David Winn of the Air Force. He had been captured about five weeks earlier and helped me greatly on the way to Hanoi.

"Upon arrival at Hoa Lo Prison (the Hanoi Hilton), I was assigned to a section we called Las Vegas. We called the different sections by different names—there was also the Sands. Without a sense of humor, you were dead."

"They placed me in solitary confinement for 16 months. . . it was like living in a closet. We were let out two or three times a day, to empty our bucket and for food, but never to exercise or communicate.

"We were never treated by the rules of the Geneva Convention. The treatment was better in 1969 and 1970; but the big improvement came in 1971. In '68, we were treated like animals.

"The torture there was for breaking regulations. . . their dumb regulations on communication with other prisoners. You were tortured into making tapes, writing a letter to the President, or a Congressman. They used our Code of Conduct as a weapon against us."

The diet in the camp in 1968 and '69 was grim. "Once a week, on Sunday mornings, we had a treat, I thought. A lot of the men hated the stuff, but I liked it. It was sticky rice, simple boiled rice with sugar thrown in. . . I'm fond of sweets."

In the fall of 1969, life began to change for the POWs.

"We were given roommates and breakfast. Our reading material was atrocious propaganda."

"In 1972, we received some decent reading material, *The Godfather, Airport,* etc. One man would read aloud to all the rest because it was so much faster and everyone wanted to hear.

"I will never forget the 18th day of December. We stood in our cells and cheered when the B-52's began hitting Hanoi. We watched the flashes long into the night from the windows as the bombing went on and on.

"We knew that the President was taking extremely drastic steps, and then the B-52 crews began coming to the camp and telling us that the war was nearly over.

"On the 20th of January 1973, there was a general announcement that we would be freed."

When Coskey returned home, there were adjustments to make to civilian life. Despite all he had been through he was just grateful to be alive. Today, he sounds humble about his survival under such conditions.

"I was a professional Navy pilot doing the job I was trained for," he says. "I got shot down and spent four and a half years in a prison—five years away from home. A lot of guys were there for seven or eight years. I wasn't there that long. And, I was just glad that I wasn't killed. Because most of the guys who were shot down were killed. Those that weren't ended up in the prison—and those were the lucky ones not the unlucky ones."

As a POW, Coskey escaped the ostracism that faced other veterans upon their return home. "We [POWs] weren't treated badly when we came home. In fact, we were treated so well that other veterans groups—from WWII and Korea—got kind of mad. The other military men [from Vietnam] returning home were not treated as well as they should have been. Whether it was a good war or not was irrelevant. They served and fought for their country. They did the right thing. But in Vietnam, they came back in dribbles and drabs, they just filtered back into the system without any parades."

Because he was so grateful to be home—alive— Coskey was able to put Vietnam behind him. To go on.

He recognizes, however, that not everyone was able to pick up the pieces as quickly and easily as he was.

For Coskey, the Wall is less of a healing force than a brilliant tribute to the brave men who lost their lives. Not a moment passes on his visits to the Wall that he doesn't feel grateful that his life was spared.

"From the first moment I saw it, I liked the design. I thought it was great—even when all the controversy surrounded it. As it turned out, it's a major attraction in the city. It's a spectacularly successful Memorial.

"The names make it successful. There's no other Memorial that has names. The rest of them are just statues or whatever. The names give it a tremendous power—like when you see people making the rubbings. It's sort of a hands-on kind of thing," he says.

"Everyone that comes in town wants to go see it. They want to go see it with a veteran because I can point out names and talk about it. That's what everybody likes." After so many years of silence surrounding Vietnam, and now, 10 years after the Wall was dedicated, there is comfort in knowing people are still talking about Vietnam. Still listening. Still making up for lost time.

"It's also impressive to see how many 58,000 names are. It's kind of scary. It's not just a number. There they are. They all died. And for what?! I've got a lot of friends that were killed in that war. I've forgotten how many now, it's been too long. But I don't have an emotional experience when I go down there. Maybe I'm too flint-hearted. I'm just glad I'm not one of the names on there."

WANDA RUFFIN

Widow of James Thomas Ruffin

In 1964, Wanda Ruffin was a newlywed, still blushing with the glow of romance. Her husband, Jim Ruffin, was a Navy pilot. Together, they celebrated their first anniversary and toasted the future. All seemed blissful.

Jim had already received his orders to go to Vietnam. He was stationed on the USS Enterprise. He was scheduled to leave for Southeast Asia in October 1964.

"We had been stationed in San Diego," recalls Wanda, "but because the Enterprise was leaving for the first time, it was leaving from the East Coast. So, they had flown all the guys who were going to be on the Enterprise from San Diego to Norfolk. I had an aunt and uncle in Norfolk, so I went to stay with them."

Before the Enterprise left for good, the squadron took it out to sea for a few weeks to make sure everything was operating smoothly.

"They were gone for a couple of weeks. During that time I went to the doctor and found out that I was pregnant. We kind of suspected it...but being so young and naive, I thought it could be anything," she says.

"I decided I wouldn't tell anybody," she continues. "I wanted him to be the first one to know. So when I went to pick him up after he got back from that short voyage, the first thing he said was 'Well what's the answer...are you?' That's all he could think about the whole time he was gone. Then we got home, and he dashed in the house and asked my aunt if he could use the phone. He picked up the phone and started calling all the relatives. I was so embarrassed," she says with a soft southern drawl.

"Fortunately, we were able to be together for our first anniversary celebration, and to celebrate that I was pregnant. A lot of the families had already said their goodbyes in San Diego," she says.

Jim and Wanda met while he was in pilot training. Jim's younger sister played matchmaker, and "hand-picked" Wanda as the special one to meet her handsome brother.

"Jim's sister was my little sister in the sorority at college," Wanda remembers. "The first night that we had a little sister party she was talking about her brother. . .you know talking about her good-looking 6'5" brother that was a Navy pilot. All the girls were saying 'I want to meet him,' and she said, 'No, I've picked him out for Wanda.' I was flattered. At the time, I was dating someone else, so I said, 'Oh no, no, no, get somebody else.' But that was before I met him!" she laughs.

They met a few months later. And married not long after.

Jim was a graduate of Auburn University. He had attended college on a Navy Scholarship. Jim loved to fly. The Navy enabled him to do what he loved. When he left on the Enterprise that October he was 24 years old. In January, he celebrated his 25th birthday. By the end of February, he'd been shot down and reported Missing in Action.

"Only a night or two before Jim was shot down, I got up early one morning and Mother was in the kitchen. And she said, 'Are you okay?' And I said, 'Yeah, why do you ask?' She said, 'Because I woke up and I couldn't go back to sleep last night, I kept thinking I was hearing you crying.' We didn't think anything about it at the time," Wanda says. Later, when they heard the bad news, they couldn't help but think the dream was more like a vision.

On that fateful day, Jim was flying an F-4, with a navigator co-pilot. Shortly after they were shot down someone reported by radio that a Yankee Pilot, or "pirate" as the enemy called them, was observed being captured. The observation took place just off the coast of where Jim's last radio contact had been.

"We felt like at least one of them had escaped from the plane before it crashed into the water," she says. "So that allowed us to hope for quite awhile.

"My first feeling was 'What am I going to do?' My whole life had been planned, or so I thought. And it all revolved around him and what we were going to do. We wrote letters to each other constantly, about our plans for when he got back," she says. "The fact that he was missing changed all that . . . it meant that he wouldn't be coming home when the others came home. And yet the fact that he was missing as opposed to being dead, gave me hope.

"In May, just about a week before my daughter was born, I received a call from my Commander's wife in San Diego. She said, 'I hope this latest news hasn't caused you to give up on Jim?' I said, 'What do you mean?' And she said, 'Well, Larry was identified as a POW.' That was the navigator aboard the plane with Jim. Then, she said, 'But that doesn't mean that just because we heard only one of them had escaped that two of them didn't.' Originally, I kept thinking: If I could just find out this much information, I'll have my answer. But even when I heard that, it didn't make me change my mind. I still kept hoping that he was alive."

Hope can carry you through the worst of times. It can also closely mirror denial. For Wanda, hope and denial became critical tools for carrying her through the pregnancy, single motherhood, and the many frustrating years ahead. "If I had had to face the fact that he was not alive at that time, I don't know if I could have done it. So I was able to go into a stage of denial, and stay there for quite a long time. Although it kept me from going on with my life, it helped me get adjusted, emotionally, for what was to come.

"In fact, we had picked out names for the baby before

it was born. If it was a boy it was to be one name, if it was a girl we had another name picked out. Yet the minute I saw her, and they said 'it's a girl,' I changed her middle name to Hope."

After Jim was reported missing, Wanda thrust herself into a whirlwind of activities to keep busy. Too busy to feel the pain.

"I lived for many years doing what I thought Jim would want me to do. After he was shot down in February, one of his sisters became ill and died. His family was going through so much. Here I had this brand new baby who was the light of our lives, and I knew that Jim would want me to be with them as much as I could...to try and help them through that very difficult time. So I spent a lot of my time with his family. My family lived about 45 miles from his family. So I divided my time between the two for a couple of years.

"Then I decided to go back to graduate school. Going to school helped me. It helped me stay busy. A lot of my friends would tease me about how I started collecting degrees. And I did. I got two graduate degrees, and finally I got a nursing degree on top of all of that," she says.

Wanda stayed active and was surrounded by family, but in many ways she was also forced into isolation. "I didn't have other wives to talk to, because we were told not to tell anyone our circumstances. We were told that if these guys were prisoners of war, any information or identification of ourselves in the press could be something that the "enemy" could use against them. That kept us from finding out about each other...and being supportive of each other as well."

Though it took a while, wives of MIAs and POWs did eventually find one another and break their code of silence. "After a couple of years I started meeting several other wives. One of the ways we would meet each other would be when pictures of POWs would come in and they would want us to identify the men in the photos," she recalls. "At that point we hadn't started talking about the issues [surrounding MIAs] but we started to at least be able to support each other."

The ability to talk with others is one of the greatest remedies for grief. Wanda says, "I think that was one of the things that was most important to me—the support I got from other families in similar circumstances.

"I continued to hope that he was alive for about four or five years," she says. "I was attending a meeting of the League of Families of POWs and MIAs in Washington. It seemed that every other wife that I would run into there, every other family member, had some kind of information...like they had either gotten a letter or had a picture or something to support their hope that their loved one was alive.

"I was becoming very frustrated over the fact that I had no evidence whatsoever, that Jim was alive. This was in May of '71. So, I went back to my hotel room that night and prayed. This is somewhat of a religious experience actually...because I had become very skeptical that there even was be a higher power. I couldn't imagine that a high power would let something like this happen—as good a person as my husband had been, for this to be happening to him, and his family, and for us to continue in limbo—it just didn't seem right. So my prayer was, 'If you exist, if there is a God, I will know. I will find out about my husband's fate. And I will know by Christmas.'

"And this was in May," she emphasizes, "so I was giving it some time. I had had long discussions about this 'higher power' issue with another POW wife. So I thought my first leap of faith was to tell her about this pact."

Wanda returned to her job in a speech therapist's office after the League of Families meeting. On her desk was a pamphlet promoting a meeting of the International Congress for the Deaf that was to be held in August. Two of the key places on the tour were Paris, where the peace talks were being held, and Sweden, where the Prime Minister who had been instrumental in providing information on POWs for many American families was.

"I looked at the pamphlet, and thought, 'Well maybe I'm supposed to go on this tour.' I figured I'd go on it, stop by and talk to the Prime Minister and go to the Paris peace talks," she says. "So, I went on the tour and visited the Prime Minister's office. He was out of the country. But his assistant pulled my husband's files. In it were all the letters I had written asking for help. He had even written to the government of North Vietnam on my behalf. But there was no real information for me.

"Then I got to Paris," Wanda recalls. "I went to the American Embassy first. I was waiting to talk to people in the embassy and there was this other woman sitting in the waiting room. We got to talking. She was from Florida and had come by herself to go to the peace talks, too. The embassy told us where the address was, and how we should get there. They told us we should take a paper that listed all the information about our husbands, in case they decided to cooperate with us."

The woman guarding the door at the peace talks was well-known for her brusque manner. She was picky regarding who she let enter and who she didn't. And she didn't care much for Americans who didn't speak French. Wanda and her new-found friend fretted over how they would handle confronting her.

"At the door, we spoke enough French that she didn't realize we didn't know the language. But she still did not let us in," she remembers. Just then, a long black car pulled up in front of the building. An Oriental man climbed out clutching a bulging briefcase. He looked important. The two women approached him and started pleading with him to help them meet the North Vietnamese delegates. They scrambled to keep up with him. As he walked through the door, they followed close behind.

"The French woman came back and started telling us we had to leave. She said she would call the police. In fact she did." But the language barrier made it impossible for the women to understand what the police wanted, and vice versa. "We just had a big communication breakdown. So they shrugged their shoulders and left. Finally, the North Vietnamese sent in a delegate who sat with us for over an hour. He kept telling us what our country was doing to his country. And we'd tell him that we weren't involved with that, that we were wives. I told him that I had a child who had been born after her father had been shot down, and she didn't know if he was alive or not. And then I said to him, 'Do you have children? How would your children feel if they didn't know if you were alive or not?' And he got tears in his eyes. Then I said, 'Just take this paper, and promise us you'll get us this information.'"

The man didn't want to take the paper. He kept waving Wanda away. Then the police returned. She once again thrust it into the man's hands. He took it from her just as they whisked Wanda up, to escort her out of the building.

That Thanksgiving, just weeks before her Christmas deadline, Wanda received a letter from the American Friends Service Committee—an anti-war group that was fed POW information from the North Vietnamese as a way to frustrate the U.S. Government. The letter contained a list of names of men Missing in Action. Beside each name was a status report. By Jim's name there was a line that read: Never detained in North Vietnam.

"And so, in a way, I thought that was my answer," she says. "I was ready to say, 'Okay, now I am a widow.' I had lived in denial up until then. And anything was better than not knowing. My daughter, who was like four years old, was saying, 'Where is my daddy?' I would say, 'Well he is either in Vietnam or he is in heaven, I don't know.' So at that point, I was ready to tell her that he was in heaven. That was one of the things I wanted to be able to do, by getting this answer.''

Wanda was still somewhat skeptical. Was this, in fact, the answer she had requested? She visited her minister and told him of her frustration. He said, ''Why don't you just ask for confirmation?'' Wanda took his advice and prayed for a confirmation. Within the next week, she received a telegram from the Prime Minister of Sweden. The telegram reported that he had been in communication with North Vietnam, and they had assured him that Jim was not a POW.

It was not until 1974 that the government actually changed Jim Ruffin's status from MIA to KIA. For Wanda, it seemed more like a formality. The final paper shuffle.

The agony she endured as a result of Vietnam lasted nearly two decades. When the first discussions of a Vietnam Veterans Memorial took place in the late 1970s, Wanda was still living life in limbo. It is frightening to realize how long overdue the Memorial was, yet to think that even then the war's hell still waged on. We had all believed its hell was behind us.

''I remember hearing that they were going to build a Memorial and that some people didn't like the design. I was in Alabama. I didn't have a lot of strong feelings about whether or not they should build one or not. One friend who was a Vietnam veteran would seek me out to tell me stuff about it. He was so thrilled and so excited. I was happy for him because it was making him happy. After the Wall was built, I can remember seeing the dedication on television. Any time it'd be on television, my eyes would hurt from trying to see if I could find my husband's name.

"Then, I remember seeing an older couple, this was on television, and the camera must have been right behind them, with the microphone right there. This older couple was touching their son's name, and the woman turned to the man, and said, 'Take off your hat.' And when he took off his hat, I lost it," she says. "Several things like that made me know that the Wall was a very moving emotional place."

While many were now able to mourn at the Wall— and seek a closure to their grief—Wanda's hell continued. One evening, a Navy car pulled up in front of her house. She and her 17-year-old daughter had been relaxing at home. When Wanda saw the car, memories of the night Jim disappeared came flooding back. She felt a knot tighten in her gut.

"It was the eeriest feeling," she explains. "They even said the same words, only this time they said his remains had been returned." It was 1983. When the remains were returned, the coldness of war came back like a slap on the face. His skeleton had been completely dismantled by the enemy. Every bone meticulously cleaned of any tissue. Then the bones were neatly stacked in a small box, not much longer than a shoe box. Having heard that remains are often returned to the wrong family, Wanda and Jim's sister requested a forensics report to prove these were Jim's remains.

"All that time, through all the experiences that I had, I was in denial. And then I went through depression, grief, and a lot of sadness. The only anger I ever felt was over the political situation. I had not felt really angry, not screaming angry, like I know is healthy. . .until one night after the visit by the forensics expert. I was looking at the materials that he had left, and I just got so angry. I got angry that they were so inhumane to my husband. I was angry at what appears to me to be such irreverent treatment of my loved one's remains. I ran through the house just banging on the Walls and screaming,'' she recalls. It was a release she had needed desperately.

"We were told that we could have him buried anywhere, in any national cemetery. I said, 'The most beautiful place, the highest honor would be for him to be buried at Arlington National Cemetery,' " she reflects. "So we were flown to Washington to go to the burial. I asked if we could go a day early so that we could go to the Wall."

Wanda and her daughter went to the Wall for the very first time together. "My daughter and I walked down to see his name. We had stopped at the directories and written down where it would be. And we got down to the proper panel, and just kind of had to scan, I guess, we didn't understand the numbering system, so we scanned the panel looking for it. It's the 5th panel from the center, so as you can imagine, it's on one of the tallest walls. When I found it, I reached up and touched it to show it to my daughter. I said, 'Here it is,' And as I said earlier, my husband was about 6'5''. . .well his name is right about at 6'6 or 7''.

"It's as if he was standing here," she told her daughter. "It would be right over his head."

"I could feel it when I touched it, I felt as if he was standing there," she says. "When I said that to her, she cried and I cried. We were standing there you know just hugging each other. And here I had thought we were on a trip that was going to be no big deal. I had not expected that going to his burial was going to be so difficult because of all the grieving that I had done in the past. But being there at the Memorial just brought it up for us. That was the first time that she and I had been emotional together."

As they stood there hugging each other, one of the volunteers was standing a few feet behind. "It was as if no one was there, but he was kind of standing off to the side watching us. Then he came up and he said, 'Are you okay? Do you need anything?' and handed us Kleenex. Later on, I reflected on how important it was, to us, for someone to be there.

"For some reason, the Wall opens people up to their feelings, it gets them in touch with them. There's something about that place that says 'It's okay to show your feelings when you are down there,'" Wanda explains. "I think that our grief over Vietnam, and over those that we lost in Vietnam was suppressed. Partly because of the way our culture handled grief at the time, and partly because of the Vietnam War and all the conflicts surrounding it. So many of us suppressed so much for so long. And when it's okay to grieve, that in itself is the greatest healing aspect. . .because people have to get their grief out.

"It also helps in that you are not just going to a lonely grave site to grieve—which is a fine place to grieve, there's nothing wrong with that—but at the Wall, you grieve in the presence of other people. People who are grieving, too, or people who are there to offer solace and comfort and say, 'Yes, I know, I understand.'

"I think that definitely helped me," she adds.

A few years after her first visit to the Wall, Wanda moved to the Washington area. When a friend from out of town came to visit, they toured the city's sights. One of their stops was the Wall.

"I saw people having the same experience I did," she says. "And I saw volunteers, Park Service volunteers, standing there helping them, handing them a Kleenex, giving them a piece of paper to do a name rubbing. And I said, 'This is so neat, I'm so glad they have these people there.' And as I started to leave, I saw this table set up near the Wall."

The table was set up for the Friends of the Vietnam Veterans Memorial, an organization that helps with the name rubbings. Wanda started talking with the man behind the table. She asked him about the volunteers...who were they...where did they come from? In no time at all, Wanda was volunteering her time down at the Wall.

"One of the first things that I noticed when I would read all the letters [requesting name rubbings] or when I would get calls, is that people would be calling, asking for help in locating someone. Veterans would be trying to locate family members of buddies that had been killed...or family members needed to talk with someone to find out if there was anything more to be learned about how that person had died. Or the children. And this is what always would get me, I guess because of my own daughter. So many children were wanting to talk with people who had served with their fathers because they were approaching their father's age. They were searching for their own identity. It always made me feel like, gosh, what if some of these people are searching for each other, and we don't even know it."

Wanda sought permission to create a form that would allow them to record the names, addresses and numbers of people with requests. A simple file drawer was created to keep track of the papers. That was the beginnings of the organization *In Touch*. As the contents of the file drawer grew, the system became less effective. Fortunately, a computer was donated to the kiosk. In 1990, a company called EDS volunteered to set up a database management system to track the names and create matches. *In Touch* had gone hi-tech.

Through *In Touch*, Wanda and the other dedicated volunteers were able to make many, many successful matches. As the news spread across the country of the heartwarming reunions taking place, Wanda herself was put in touch with someone special.

The ABC news magazine program 20/20 interviewed Wanda about her work with the Wall and the *In Touch* program. Shortly after the interview aired, she received a phone call. The man calling wanted to know if

Wanda's husband was in fact, Lt. Jim Ruffin. She said that yes, Jim was her husband. The man told her that he was stationed with Jim on the USS Enterprise.

"He and I were in Bible study and choir together," the man told Wanda. He also told her that he had gone down to Jim's stateroom the night before he took off for the last time. The two young men had been practicing a song for the choir. They got to talking for a while. Finally, Jim said he had to go to bed early because he had an early flight in the morning.

"What time do you have to be up?" he asked, and Jim told him the flight time. The next morning, the man got up early just to see Jim off.

"That was just so neat, to me, that he had seen him off," Wanda says. But there was even more behind this story. Apparently, Wanda's daughter had been dreading the day she would outlive her father. On June 18th of that year, she would be the exact age he was when he died, 25 years, two months and two days. This date was extremely significant to her—more so than even her own birthday.

"I knew that she was dreading it," Wanda says. "Both of us dreaded it. Because she had said things to me like, 'If I live to be as old as my father.' I knew that this was going to be a difficult time for her. Well, the day that I heard from this man was June 17th. He was calling on the eve of the day. . .the eve of the day she would be her father's age. . .and the fact that this man had been with Jim on the eve before his final flight. I told him the story and neither one of us could believe it. I asked if he wouldn't mind talking to my daughter. And he said he'd be honored.

"That night, close to midnight before it would have been June the 18th, she called me. And I had said, 'Call me no matter what, I want to know how you are.' And so she called me, and said 'I'm going to be okay. It's going to be okay now.' And I realized that if it were not for the Memorial, all of these means of helping people would not have been available. Helping others has become the focus of the healing. And it was all this, you know, if it was not for this work. . . if I were not one of the parties involved with the Wall and with this program, we ourselves would not have had this blessing.''

And indeed, to feel healed is to feel blessed.

A VETERAN'S CHILD

Today many of the children born to Vietnam veterans are in their 20s—about the same age many of their fathers were when they served. When you talk to them, you are struck by how young they really are. Ironically, some are now older than their fathers ever were. The average age of the soldiers killed in Vietnam was 19.

In talking to these young adults, you are also struck by how little they know about their fathers. Their curiosity is only now being piqued. They are beginning to look out beyond their own world. They are growing up. And becoming more curious about who their fathers were, what they were like, and how they were killed. For those who are fortunate enough to visit the Wall, that experience often rips the lid off their inquisitiveness.

Sean Purcell was only 16 months old when his father, Michael Joseph Purcell, was shot down. It was April 1, 1968. One day earlier his mother had given birth to his sister. In one 24-hour period, the family received the brightest and the darkest news there is in life.

Today, Sean is attending law school. He has boyish appeal and smiling Irish eyes. His mother says he's a lot like his father. To prove it, she shows him pictures every time he visits home. Sean just turned 25. The same age his father was in 1968.

Michael Purcell was a Navy flier, a navigator. In college he joined the ROTC program. After he graduated in 1966, he went in for active duty. By late 1967, he received his orders for Vietnam.

"We never really talk about it [their father's death] very much to tell you the truth," Sean says. "Among the three of us—my mother, sister, and I—I guess it's come out more, recently, now that we're older. I guess it was kind of difficult since my mother remarried. It was never really brought up in like a family context or anything. I think she [his mother] really wants to talk about it, but it is kind of a difficult subject.''

For many Vietnam widows, the grief and pain of losing their husbands was too much heartache to endure. The only way to cope was to ignore the pain and move on with their lives. Shortly after Sean's sister reached school-age, his mother pursued a Master's Degree. She also remarried around that same time.

''It was very important to her, when she remarried, that my sister and I keep my father's name,'' he remembers.

Yet even though there was now a stable family life for Sean and his sister, he says, ''When I was younger, I always felt out of place. I felt like I was the only one who didn't have my original parents or something. As I got older, there were more and more people whose parents were divorced. But I rarely ever encountered someone whose father was dead, until college.

''Now that I'm older, I've met other kids whose fathers were killed in Vietnam from time to time. With the ones I've met, it's kind of like a silent . . .you know, you just kind of know how that person feels,'' he says.

In 1979 when talk of the Memorial began, Sean was only 12 years old. ''I don't really remember anything about it. I took a trip to Washington when I was in high school, like a school trip, but I don't even recall going there. I don't think we did. I guess I really didn't know about it until I moved here for college in 1985,'' he says.

Sean remembers well his first time to the Wall. ''Actually it was kind of upsetting. It was my freshman year in college, at the end of a long night of drinking. It was like 4:30 in the morning, and a bunch of us went down. There were some people there who had relatives that were killed, and we kind of looked at it, and all had an emotional type reaction. Since everything had been kind of buried in my family, not really buried, but rather not talked about, I hadn't had much cause to think about it that much. But visiting the Wall really made me think about it." For Sean, that visit made him want to learn more. "Before, I sometimes wondered what my father would have been like or what things would have been like. But I had never really allowed myself to think about it too much. Since I've been down there, I've wondered a lot more. Before I guess I just didn't really want to deal with it at all. Now I'm more receptive when my mom starts showing me pictures and stuff.

"It's scary. . . I just recently realized that, now at this age—because a lot of the pictures were taken of him when he was my age—we do have a very striking physical resemblance which I never really noticed before. And my mom tells me that a lot of my mannerisms are very similar to his.

"Last year I ended up calling my mom out of the blue—not even realizing it was my father's birthday—and she was like 'It's really strange that you should call. . .'"

Since his first visit to the Wall, Sean visits fairly often now. "I guess every few months I find myself down there. A little bit more recently because I've started bicycling a lot, so I tend to ride towards the monuments, and I'll stop by," he says. "I wind up going at night. I think it's much more awe-striking at night than in the day. And I generally don't like to go there with other people. Last weekend my stepsister and her boyfriend were in town, and I took them down to the monuments and stuff, but I didn't really feel comfortable taking them there. I don't feel comfortable just hanging out and being reflective when I'm taking somebody sightseeing."

Enabling him to reflect is perhaps the largest impact the Wall has had on Sean. "In my own mind the Wall had something to do with how I came to start thinking about things a little more," he explains. "Plus, I think it was also my age and basically coming to grips with things myself. I've always been the type of person who buries things and doesn't worry about them. But recently I've found it helps to talk about things. And maybe that'll help open up a few new channels of communication with my sister and my mom. But mostly, the Wall helped open up my mind to wondering who my father was. . ."

Like Sean, Christine Hess was an infant when her father, Frederick W. Hess Jr., was reported missing in action in March 1969. He was an Air Force pilot. He and his co-pilot ejected from their plane. The co-pilot was rescued and reported that he saw Hess' parachute open. But he never saw Hess land. In 1979, after being reported missing for 10 years, his status was changed by the U.S. Government to KIA.

On Memorial Day, 1974, Christine attended her first ceremony held for the children of veterans killed or missing in action, hosted by *No Greater Love*. "I remember I was just about seven [years old]. It was a very pretty sunny day. It was exciting because I knew I was doing something important. I knew it had to do with my father and I was happy to be there," Christine recalls. But she had no real concept of the importance of such ceremonies.

Christine grew up in the Washington, D.C., area, and continued to be a part of special remembrances through *No Greater Love*. She was one of the children who participated at the dedication ceremony of the Wall in 1982.

"I remember I was a high school sophomore," she says. "I really didn't know too much about what was going on. I didn't recognize the significance of it. I remember sitting up on stage and looking out at this crowd of people and thinking, 'Wow, this is really something to a lot of other people.' But at the time I just really didn't have a feel for what it was all about.

"I felt that way until I was about 14 or 15 years old.

Then I started noticing the people coming to the ceremonies were often veterans, and men in wheelchairs. That's when I started thinking, 'Oh, well this has a lot more serious impact.'

"During the dedication ceremony, we had different people stand up and read something off a card about what our part was and why we were there. I explained I was a child of someone who was missing, and that his name was on the Wall with a special symbol."

Like other families who lost a loved one in Vietnam, Christine and her mother tried to get on with their lives. But unlike others, having a loved one declared missing forces you to live life in limbo. "When I was a kid, I used to pretend he'd come back," she says. "That seems kind of silly now. I guess the realist in me wants to say that it's been so many years, chances are he's gone. But then you always have that question mark in your mind."

Christine also remembers feeling somewhat out-of-place without her father around. What bothered her most, and still does, was having to explain what happened. "I hate going into this long drawn-out explanation. Like even today, I talk about my mother and people ask 'What about your father?' And I have to tell this long, long drawn-out story. I don't necessarily try and avoid it, but it's such a strange thing to even bring up, discuss and explain. I just think of it as me and my mother now."

Still as each year passes, Christine becomes intrigued to know more about the war and about who her father was. "I think I've become that way, even just within the last year," she explains. "I guess it's because now I'm getting older and I'm used to being on my own. And when you think that I'm about 25, and he was 27. That's really weird. It just blows my mind to think that he was just a couple of years older than I am . . . and he had a family and then just disappeared.

"From pictures I've seen, I look a lot like him. From

what my mother and other people have told me, personality-wise I seem to be a lot like him. I guess somewhat of an easygoing type of person. And so was he.''

For Christine, it has been helpful to meet others whose lives have been similarly affected by the events in Vietnam. Meeting someone who truly understands the loss, pain, sadness and frustration can be an important aspect of a person's healing. Through activities sponsored by *No Greater Love* and *Sons and Daughters In Touch*, Christine has made some valuable new friendships.

"In October of last year, Carmella had another tree-planting ceremony, and I went to that. I became pretty good friends with another girl whose dad was killed in action. This is still kind of a new friendship, and a lot of this is still kind of sinking in. But through her I've become involved with a group called *Sons and Daughters In Touch*. I just went to my first meeting last Monday, and I'm designing a T-shirt for them for the Father's Day ceremony at the Wall,'' she says.

Sons and Daughters In Touch grew out of another group called *In Touch*, which brings together visitors to the Wall. *In Touch* has helped reunite veterans, introduce the families of veterans on the Wall to one another, and acts as a link for anyone wishing to contact someone who has a loved one on the Wall.

When Christine visits the Wall, she usually goes with a friend. Often, she'll ride her bike on the trails leading to it. She appreciates the Wall's simple and striking design. "As an architect, I may be somewhat biased, but I like the color: black. I like black. All my furniture is black,'' she laughs. "I like the way it's a shiny surface. I like the texture of the surface. My favorite thing, I guess, is that everyone's name is there. That took so many hours of craftsmanship. It is a very beautiful piece of work.

"When I think of the Wall,'' she continues,

"I always think of reflections...reflections of the setting sun...or the monument...and the Lincoln Memorial somewhat behind it. I've seen people get very emotional, I've seen people come and lay flowers. I'm glad that it marks something that was a very big part in history and that was a very big part of many people's lives...but I think it means more to people that were older, ones that went through the experience 20 years ago." Maybe. Even still, you can't help picture her 10 years from now, standing proudly before the Wall, a small child's hand pressed softly in hers, telling Grandpa's story.

hear about the medical staff. You should get more out of the Vietnam War, some of it...

REUNITED

The Wall has brought many long-lost buddies together. Some have met again at the Wall. Others have sought to rekindle a friendship after visiting the Wall. Here is the story of two veterans brought together by the Wall.

Around the holidays in 1985, Shaun Sheehan received this letter.

Dear Shaun,

While reading the book, *To Heal A Nation*, by Jan Scruggs and Joel Swerdlow, I saw your name mentioned. The fact that you were a Marine Infantry Officer during the Vietnam conflict was also mentioned. If you are the officer I remember, you were an Artillery FO. You were also in the Vietnam Theater of Operations during the Tet Offensive of 1968, and subsequent to those months.

In addition, you served as an Artillery FO during April–May 1968, with Alpha Co., 1st Bn., 7th Mar., 1st Mar. Div. on an operation 20 clicks south of Da Nang on Go Noi Island. During that operation, we operated with a company from the 26th Marines whose company commander was Captain Charles Robb, currently Governor of Virginia, and son-in-law of ex-President Lyndon B. Johnson. During the operation, the company you were attached to had a Commanding Officer named Captain Bill R. I was the Company Gunnery Sergeant of that same unit.

One evening we chased an NVA Regiment into the mountains southeast of Go Noi and had to spend the evening on the mountain. You, your radio operator, and I spent the night lying on the poncho with one above us (it had started to rain) while we shivered. There were knees knocking and teeth chattering until dawn.

Well Shaun, if you are the officer I knew, I would

consider it a pleasure to hear from you. Please either drop me a line or give me a call.

Sincerely,

Jim P.
Sergeant Major, Marines (Ret)

Shaun was the officer the Sergeant Major remembered. As the New Year of 1986 began, Shaun contacted the Sergeant Major telling him that he was in fact the man shivering on the mountain. In no time, he received another letter.

Dear Shaun,

It was a pleasant shock to see your name mentioned in the book *To Heal A Nation*, but a fantastic pleasure to renew an association I considered special. Special not only due to the evening on the mountain, but the day the Huey gunships took us under fire and you jumped up on one of those burial mounds to wave them off; and for the day you expressed everyone's feelings at the battalion staff meeting. At the battalion meeting you told the Personnel Officer, "I'll give you a nickel for every time you have been outside the wire, and you wouldn't have a dollar's worth of change." You were always outspoken and fearless of exposing yourself to danger to get the job done; you were an inspiration. My knowledge of you makes it easy to understand the attainment of the lofty position you now hold.

In 1969 neither of us had a family. The family I have is indicative of how the years have faded into the past. I now have three sons, 16, 14, and 10. Whenever I see my boys it reminds me of the guys who had sons and daughters while in country and never got to hold them in their arms. Those boys and girls are 17 years old now. Often I have found myself desiring to meet those children, to tell them about their father, and to hold them in my arms for the men.

You mentioned your work with the Vietnam Veterans Memorial in Washington. It so happens that my reason for reading the book *To Heal A Nation* was to obtain ideas which could help me in raising funds to defray the cost of a monument planned for construction in South Carolina. Thus far, the response, enthusiasm and positive attitudes of all I have contacted to support our endeavor has been fantastic. Patriotism is (again) alive and well in these United States. After all these years it even amazed me at the tremendous emotional involvement I have with all the men and women with whom we served. It is like a bittersweet visit to the past.

I surely hope your Christmas was one of joy and that the New Year will present challenges, worthwhile and enjoyable, and rewarding to you and yours. Again it has been great hearing from you and I intend to visit with you sometime next year. God love you and your family in the unending manner familiar only to Him.

Your fellow Marine,
Jim

Though life goes on, memories remain. Some friendships can endure a lifetime when based on mutual respect, trust, and faith. The kind of feelings you develop, side by side, in combat.

PHIL SCRUGGS

When Jan Scruggs returned from Vietnam, he lived for a short while with his brother's family. Phil, Jan's nephew, was just a boy. The two developed a close bond.

During the time Jan was spearheading the Vietnam Veterans Memorial project, Phil was overseas. Occasionally, he heard progress reports through the family grapevine. But the vision behind the Memorial was foreign to him.

When Phil returned to the States in 1987, Jan went with him on his first visit to the Wall.

"I had a hard time with it because I didn't know what Vietnam was...I didn't understand it. It was something people didn't really talk about and still don't in many ways. My parents didn't talk about it. I never learned about it in school. But I really had a passion for history," Phil says.

So, he studied up on the Vietnam conflict and started learning more about the intimate details of the Wall. As friends would come to visit him in Washington, he would play tour guide. One summer, a friend visiting from Switzerland was interested in finding out if her last name appeared on the Wall. As they were flipping through one of the directories, Phil glanced across the table and noticed a casualty listing the same day he was born, August 18, 1965. It had a tremendous impact on him. He went to the Wall and found the man's name.

He wanted to know more. "This guy died the day I was born and I didn't know anything about why he died," he explains. "So, I did a little bit of research and started talking with some of the volunteers. I learned August 18th was the first day of Operation Starlight in Vietnam. It was the first real combat action that the Marines were involved in. Forty-eight men were killed.

It was a six-day operation.

"It just really hit me," he continues. "That day they lost their lives. . .and I was given mine. That really means something to me."

As Phil spent more and more time down at the Wall, learning all he could about the men listed, the other volunteers invited him to join them. He agreed. It seemed the perfect opportunity for him to share his growing knowledge with others.

"I really felt it important for other people to know this information, too. . . I felt, in a sense, that I owed it to the guys that died the day I was born," he says.

There are distinct reasons why people visit the Wall. Some go to mourn. Some to pay their respects. Others visit out of curiosity.

In many ways, each volunteer has his or her own motive for spending time down at the Wall. Those who lost someone dear are often there to help visitors cope with their overwhelming emotions. These volunteers know instinctively how to comfort. They are also extremely protective of the visitors who are overcome with grief and sorrow.

There are other volunteers who are veterans. They are uniquely qualified to console veterans who visit. Phil recognizes he is not qualified for membership in this elite club.

His main desire is to help educate the curiosity seeker. The stranger to Vietnam. If more and more people become educated about Vietnam, particularly the young adults of his generation who were too young to remember details, then he feels the 58,000 plus deaths will not have been in vain.

Phil's knowledge about Vietnam, particularly the historical aspects, is vast. He can spout statistics, dates, and details for hours. For as long as a visitor can ask questions, Phil can answer. Their most common response is, "I had no idea. . ."

Nearly every visitor is struck silent by the awesomeness of the Wall. "You can see the difference, just by standing at the Lincoln Memorial," he says. "There are kids running around, adults flashing cameras. Then you go down to the Wall (which is only a short walk away) and it's a totally different atmosphere. When you go down there you lose your sense in time. It's very much a park within a park, just as it was designed to be. You can lose yourself and lose touch with the outside world."

As a volunteer, Phil and others have the special opportunity to witness many heartwarming moments. On one such moment, a volunteer was at the computer in the kiosk trying to help a man find a name. The veteran didn't really know who he was looking for. He was relying on faded memories. But he remembered the details surrounding the situation. So, he began to describe it aloud. He had found a badly wounded soldier, who was not from his unit, in a combat zone. The veteran picked him up, carried him a great distance, and put him in a helicopter. At the time, he had no idea whether the soldier was alive or not. And the veteran couldn't recall the exact date.

On the other end of the kiosk another veteran was being helped by a different volunteer. He described how he had been badly wounded, and somebody had picked him up and brought him to a helicopter. He felt he owed his life to this guy and he really needed to find him.

It didn't take long to realize that these veterans were telling two versions of the same story.

There are other times when volunteers must simply speak through a soft, reassuring touch. Like a gentle hand on the shoulder.

"One time," Phil remembers, "it was around dusk, and there was this man just standing there looking at the Wall. He was obviously a veteran by the way he was dressed. He had a fatigue jacket on. He was just standing there for about an hour. I usually don't approach people.

I mean I can tell when they want their space. It's something I've learned. But he was down there for awhile. I finally walked over and just kind of sat next to him and looked up to the Wall where he was staring. I felt him looking at me. He said, 'That's my Wall, that's my section. I was in the Green Berets on the Cambodian border with a squad of 12 men. I was in charge of that squad for six months and that squad never got bigger than 12 men...and I went through 54 men. Those are their names.'"

"That's all he said," Phil remembers. "I didn't say anything. I think he just felt relieved to have told his story to me. Then, unfortunately, a group of kids from a tour bus came by. He just kind of looked at them, and with a very sad face said, 'They'll never know.' Then he turned around and walked off."

Leaving mementos at the Wall is a common ritual. On Veterans Day, 1989, Phil spent several hours volunteering at the Wall. He spent most of his time collecting the artifacts. He would start at one end, slowly collecting the items, logging them in, and carefully placing them in protective bags. By the time he would reach the opposite end of the Wall, he would look back and the entire space would again be filled with mementos. For nine straight hours he collected items.

At one point that day, he had cleared an area of one panel. He had turned away for a second. As he turned back, a wedding ring was resting gently against the black granite path beside the Wall. There was no note. Only the ring.

For all its ability to heal, Phil is most pleased with the awareness the Wall has prompted. It has opened our eyes.

"The best thing to me, is that more people are aware of Vietnam. I think we will still need to recognize veterans of Vietnam, and destroy that negative stereotype of who they are. A lot of veterans that I see down there and speak with are not like the images in people's minds. They come down in business suits, clean shaven, very professional. They have families, wives, and kids," he says.

For Phil, the Wall is a place that provides a great sense of personal fulfillment. "I do a lot of volunteer work with different organizations. But the Wall is the first place where I felt totally unselfish. I felt that I could really help in a serious way. I could go down there in a bad mood, and even though the Wall can sometimes seem sad, helping people find names, helping them to understand Vietnam, and understand why it was fought, gives me a great deal of satisfaction. It just means so much. For instance, one woman asked me to do a rubbing of a name, and I did. She looked at me with a tear in her eye, and said he was her son. Then she turned around and hugged me, and thanked me for being there. That means so much. And that kind of experience makes it so hard to leave at the end of the day."

IN TOUCH

Through programs associated with the Wall, like the *In Touch* program, people who have never met have been brought together, bonded by their ties to Vietnam. Here is one of those stories, told to me by Wanda Ruffin, organizer of the *In Touch* program.

A man sent an application to the *In Touch* offices, asking for help in locating the relatives of a man he served with in Vietnam. Unfortunately he didn't even know the man's first name. He thought he was from Flint, Michigan, and guessed that his last name was Luna.

On the application he wrote, "This man saved my life, not once but twice. It's time I told his family of my respect for him."

There was something about his letter that struck Wanda. She developed a personal interest in his request and tried to help as best she could.

"I used our computer to find out the casualty dates matching all the Lunas on the Wall," she explains. "Then I checked the locations of where they were killed. I was able to get information on several Lunas. I called the man who submitted the request and together we went through the information. We picked out which Luna we thought it was. . .and it turned out he was from Flint, Michigan."

Wanda then called Flint, Michigan, and discovered there were 25 to 30 Luna families in the area. An *In Touch* volunteer in Flint, who was also an EDS employee (the company that developed the computerized match system for the Wall), agreed to do some checking around to try to narrow down the field.

Afraid to seem intrusive by calling these families, the girl devised a postcard that described their effort and asked for a reply. Then, she mailed them off to each of the families in Flint.

A nephew of the man whose name is on the Wall walked into her office with the letter in his hand.

"He was so excited to have heard from her," Wanda recalls, "that he couldn't even put it in the mail. He had to deliver it in person. And it turns out that most of the 30 or so Luna families are all related to each other. So it's a huge family."

EDS paid the travel expenses for the veteran from Texas to visit the entire clan. Ninety members of the Luna family gathered together in a hotel room to greet him (the crowd was too large to fit in someone's home).

As he walked in the room, a beautiful Hispanic woman, the family's matriarch, presented him with a dozen red roses. "Thank you, we want to thank you for remembering Adolpho," the woman said. Adolpho was her son.

Throughout the night, the veteran told story after story about Adolpho. And he told them about how Adolpho had saved his life. On two occasions.

The man had come to pay his respects. To say thanks. Only to be greeted with open arms, by a family grateful that someone remembered their son.

MISSING

"I love to talk about my dad," Beth Stewart says as we get comfortable in her Washington, D.C., apartment. She's a vivacious woman who talks easily and eagerly about her father's plight in Vietnam.

"Dad was a career Air Force officer," she begins. "All he wanted to do was fly."

Pete Stewart was born in Glasgow, Scotland, and came to the United States at an early age. From the time he was young he dreamed of being a pilot. He tried to join up early on but was turned down because of a lazy eye. Figuring the Royal Canadian Air Force might accept him, he moved north. They gave him a regimen of exercises for his eye to help him strengthen the muscles. In no time, he had corrected the problem.

He returned to New York, just as World War II broke out. The demand for fliers was high. Pete was quickly accepted and went on to serve in both World War II and Korea.

As Vietnam began, he again wanted to serve his country. On August 2, 1965, he left to go overseas. He hugged his wife Marnie and their six children goodbye.

On March 15, 1966, his plane was shot down.

"He was stationed in Thailand," Beth explains. "He was flying on a reconnaissance mission over Vietnam. There were two planes. He was in the number two plane. He was the backseater. Oddly enough he took someone else's place that day. There was a visiting dignitary, the officer who was to fly that day, had to meet with. Dad offered to take his place."

"Anyway," she continues, "the two planes were basically looking for targets in North Vietnam. Dad's plane saw a truck which they suspected to be carrying ammunition. So they signalled to the first plane that they had seen the target and that they were coming around to go over the target. They did. And Dad's plane went down over it. That's the last contact the number one plane had with my dad's plane. Except that shortly after, they did see an explosion on the ground. But he [the pilot in plane No. 1] doesn't know whether it was the bombs hitting the target or if it was my dad's plane."

There was some indication that the pilots survived the shoot-down. A red star flare was fired shortly after the explosion.

"That afternoon, March 15th, I came home from school. I was just two months shy of turning 12 years old. I was running upstairs to change clothes to run right back outside," Beth remembers. "And there was a knock at the door. I opened the door and there were two men in uniform. They asked to see Mother. It doesn't dawn on you right then as a child that something terrible is getting ready to happen. So I ran upstairs to get Mom, and told her that there were two men at the door. That's when I saw the expression on her face. And I knew that something really terrible was going to happen.

"Her face went ashen," she recalls. "And she said to tell them that she would be there in a minute. She was lying down at the time, and she said 'Please let them know I'll be right down.' So I did. Then, she came on down, and I hid on the stairway to listen to everything they had to say. I'll never forget them taking Mother's arm and saying 'But Marnie, he's only missing.' And now you've got to understand, it's 26 years later and he's still 'only missing,'" she says caustically.

"When you are told that someone is missing, as a child, you don't understand. You simply cannot comprehend what that means," she says. "We'd go to school, and kids would say 'What does your dad do?' Well for five years, I kept telling everybody my dad was in Vietnam. Sooner or later, they started saying, 'Well when is he coming home Beth? It's been five years.' But

I wasn't going to say he was dead, because he wasn't. I had no reason to believe that he was dead."

For Marnie Stewart, coping meant having faith in the military that they were doing everything they could. Just like they said they were. And it meant carrying on. Raising six young children. Alone. She moved the family to Florida, where she had been raised.

For years the family kept hoping for some word. Some sign about the fate of Pete Stewart.

"In 1973, when the first planeloads of prisoners came home, you would sit there, and probably every MIA family will tell you this, you sat there watching every man that got off that plane. You wanted there to be one more person behind them," she remembers, "and you wanted it to be Dad. You never missed a face, you watched every one. But Dad didn't come home."

In 1975 the family received a call from the Air Force asking them to examine some photographs of American prisoners of war.

"Mother immediately picked out the picture of my dad. We said, 'That's Pete Stewart. No question about it.' We identified him, each in turn, independently. The Air Force came back about 30 days later and they said 'Well sorry, it's not your father. We've identified it as another flier.'"

The Stewart family wasn't so convinced. "We knew it to be Dad and it never shook our conviction that it was Dad. But what can you do?" she says. What they did was confront the men the Air Force claimed were in the picture. Both denied the picture was of them. Armed with this information, Beth went back to the Air Force. Still they stonewalled her, saying they didn't care what the men claimed, the picture was not her father.

"You have to understand, if they had a picture of someone who did not come home, what happened to him? They [the U.S. Government] weren't going to have that situation," she says.

Years passed and still the military would not divulge any information about Pete Stewart's whereabouts or the photograph.

"In 1984 my mother and I came up here to a National League of Families meeting. I had graduated from law school at that time, and I had a practice in Florida." she says. "Honestly, I came up here because I had never been to Washington, D.C. I thought, well they fly you in for free, so why not visit. Mother wanted to come because she wanted to attend the meeting. Well, I went to a meeting of sons and daughter of MIAs and they told me more about my dad and his case than the U.S. Government had ever told me. I was flabbergasted. I went back home, and started digging, and digging, and digging, and digging. It became so apparent to me that the American public did not know that these men were still alive. And we had to do something quickly to get them home."

Beth's belief that her father and other prisoners of war were still being held alive in Vietnam prompted her to close her Florida law practice and move to Washington, D.C., to be closer to the powers that could make things happen. Hers is a controversial belief. But when you listen to her reasons for believing and hear the conviction in her voice, you can't help wondering yourself.

Beth's crusade continued. Still, she made no headway. Finally, after a nationally televised program aired on which she accused the military of withholding information about her father, there was a breakthrough.

She received confirmation in the mail that it was her father in the photograph. The picture was taken in 1969 by a Japanese group. It was finally confirmation that Pete Stewart had survived the shoot-down for at least three years.

"It's real hard to think of him going through this," she says. "This is the last photograph that I have of him...and it's of a man holding a gun to him, marching him along. But I know my dad, and he's as tough as they come and very committed. If there was anyway for him to survive, he would.''

In her search for answers, Beth has poured over intelligence documents. "In one, they don't say my dad's name, but they mention the location where he went down. And there is evidence of sightings of live American POWs all up and down the region there. One report that sticks in my mind mentions a man they [the North Vietnamese villagers] call Colonel. The report is he's just an old man, and he can't move very well because he's older. They say the villagers try and take care of him.'' When Pete Stewart was shot down, he was a Lieutenant Colonel. He has since been made a Colonel. Today, he would be in his late 70s.

"The first time I saw the Wall was in 1984, on that trip with my mother. So, it was also the first time I learned about Americans in Southeast Asia that were still alive. It was the first time that I learned that my father, and all of these men, had been abandoned and left over there,'' she recalls. "So all of this was going through my mind. My mother and I came down to the Wall. That was difficult because our family simply did not talk about my father a lot because it hurt. We didn't sit down at the table, and say 'Dad would have liked this' or 'Dad would have liked that.' It's not that you didn't stop thinking about him, but to talk about him was very painful, to this day it's painful. We each remembered Dad in our own way. But it hurt so much, because there were too many unanswered questions.

"So when I was at the Wall with my mother, that is a time that Mother and I shared together with my dad. And it was a very special time. I could never say in words what that Wall means to me. I will try because it's important that other people understand just what that Wall does mean,'' she emphasizes.

"That first trip down to the Wall stirred up a number

of things inside of me. Because of what I was learning it added to the emotions, but I also had a stronger conviction that my father survived. So, here I was before a wall with his name on it, a Memorial honoring him. That feels good to me. I want my father to be honored. But I also want him to come home. . .and to see his name on that Wall."

As she spoke, her words pierced the air. It was a chilling thought.

"People call the Wall a healing wall. I feel it's more like a living wall because inside your heart your loved one lives. When I go, there is a bond between me and one name out of 58,000 on that Wall. . .a bond that is so strong. I speak to my father from my heart to his heart.

"When I go down there, I go down there on March 15th, August 12th, November 11th. March 15th was my dad's shoot down date. August 12th is his birthday. November 11th is my mother and father's wedding anniversary. . .and it's also Veterans Day. Every time I go down there, I leave my dad's picture, a picture of the family. . .I leave a message to him, and a message to the visitors to the Wall letting them know that my father survived, and we've got to get him home. And I leave flowers from all of the family. A yellow rose from Mother, a double delight rose from my grandmother, who always kept a double delight by his picture on the piano, and I leave flowers from each of the children.

"On the flyer that I leave, I tell the world that 'Today is Col. Peter J. Stewart's birthday, he will spend it again as a POW'. . .or it will say, 'Today is Marnie and Pete Stewart's wedding anniversary. She's waiting for him to come home.' It says, 'This is my father, here he is alive, let's get him home,' and I always take down a biography of Dad, with the circumstances surrounding the shoot-down, the circumstances surrounding the picture [of him as a POW], and I take 100 or so copies.

"Then I ask the park volunteer not to collect the mementos too early. I say, 'Please make sure it stays all day and all night.' They are very good about it. Then I stand back against the chain, behind the fence, and I watch everybody come by. They always stop, you know. They read all of the mementos that are down there, and they stop and they look at this poster, they look at this picture of Pete Stewart, they look up and see his name on the Wall. And I sit there, watching as they explain it to each other. You watch a parent tell a child, you watch a Vietnam veteran tell his spouse, you watch a teacher tell a student, and you watch a friend tell a friend. And they explain, especially a parent to a child, 'This sign says this man served his country, went over to Vietnam, was shot down, he was taken prisoner, and he has not come home.'"

Beth pauses, collecting her thoughts. "For a moment in time, these people from all over the country remember Pete Stewart. They care about Pete Stewart. And it is the most precious thing to me. They will have no idea what that means to me, standing behind them, and watching them gesture to one another about him. To see them look at his name, read about him, look at his picture, and know that Pete Stewart exists. . .that's very important to me. For that alone, I will be eternally grateful to that Wall."

REFLECTIONS—10 YEARS AFTER

By Jan Scruggs

"The Wall" is now 10 years old. What is it about anniversaries that makes one remember and reflect? Perhaps we need such historic benchmarks to remind us of the significance of events. Maybe we need these milestones in our lives to remember what is important to us as individuals.

The Vietnam Veterans Memorial has been the most important part of my life and will likely be the most significant achievement I shall ever attain. It is difficult to express the satisfaction I feel at having been able to bring about a national Memorial engraved with the names of all those whose lives were lost during the war in Vietnam.

Many people helped bring about what was once thought of as an impossible dream. More than 300,000 Americans contributed money. Veterans, school children, former antiwar protesters. Organizations such as the American Legion, Veterans of Foreign Wars, labor unions, and business groups contributed. Hundreds of volunteers from around the country gave generously of their time. Members of our Board of Directors and our staff have served the project well.

There are so many warm memories. I remember one special moment from the summer of 1981—a naval officer in uniform visited the Memorial's construction site. He brought with him a Purple Heart. The medal, he explained, belonged to his brother, who was a carrier pilot killed in action while on a mission near Hanoi. He gently placed his brother's Purple Heart in the concrete foundation being poured for the Memorial.

The Memorial was dedicated November 13, 1982. In the one week the Memorial was open prior to its formal dedication, Americans came to visit from throughout the country. They left behind hundreds and hundreds of items—a pair of cowboy boots, teddy bears, photographs, medals. These items all had one thing in common—each represented a link with someone who gave his or her life in Vietnam. More than 26,000 items have now been left at the Memorial.

Where else in the world do pilgrims leave personal treasures such as these? The answer: there is no other such place—in America or anywhere else in the world. It was this that led me to create *The Wall That Heals*. My hope is that this humble book has helped you feel the power of the Memorial through the stories of people touched by the Wall.

The Wall has touched me in a positive way. My life can never be the same again. Once the Memorial was finished, I became an attorney and a successful motivational speaker. I tell audiences the amazing story of the Memorial; I hope to inspire others to have the courage to try to change things. Whether the problem is helping the homeless or cleaning up the environment, solutions only happen when we, as individuals, decide to get involved. Giving people the courage to take that first step is so satisfying.

Visit the Memorial. It is your Memorial. Visit the names. The names, like the Memorial, belong to you. For the names are those of men and women who—like you—were born in this magnificent land we call America...this land we call home. They fought for you as did their forefathers in places like Guadalcanal, Inchon, Gettysburg, Lexington, and Concord. We owe them all a debt that can never be repaid.

Future generations will look at the names engraved on the Memorial and ask, "Why did these people die in Vietnam?" The Wall will help answer this question. Because it will remind Americans of our history—and of the sacrifices made by those who served—for as long as our nation exists.

VISITING THE VIETNAM
VETERANS MEMORIAL

National Park Service Rangers as well as volunteers are on hand to assist visitors at the Vietnam Veterans Memorial in Washington, D.C. They will be happy to answer questions about the Wall, help locate names, do name rubbings, etc.

Financial contributions help preserve and protect the Wall. Donations also support major commemorative events such as the 10th Anniversary. Please send any gifts to:

VVMF
1360 Beverly Road
Suite 300
McLean, Virginia 22101